SALVATI
AND ROMA

SALVATION, THE BIBLE, AND ROMAN CATHOLICISM

WILLIAM WEBSTER

THE BANNER OF TRUTH TRUST

THE BANNER OF TRUTH TRUST

Head Office
3 Murrayfield Road
Edinburgh
EH12 6EL
UK

North America Sales
PO Box 621
Carlisle
PA 17013
USA

banneroftruth.org

First published 1990
Reprinted 2001, 2009, 2018

*

ISBN
Print: 978 0 85151 571 7

*

*

Typeset in 10.5/12 Linotron Plantin

Printed in the USA by
Versa Press Inc.,
East Peoria, IL.

Contents

APPENDICES

Introduction

Some time ago I was in earnest conversation with a very devout Roman Catholic. We were discussing specific teachings of the Roman Catholic Church. When I mentioned a particular doctrine this person stated very emphatically, 'But the Church doesn't teach that any more.'

That greatly surprised me. I was raised in the Roman Catholic Church. I attended parochial schools until I was thirteen years old, and a Benedictine monastery throughout my high school years. I was well schooled in basic Roman Catholic doctrine and teaching. But in the face of this assertion I found myself questioning whether the Church had indeed changed its position in the specific area we had been discussing. I was aware that many changes had been initiated within the Church as a result of Vatican II. Perhaps some of its major doctrinal positions had also changed?

Some time later I was reading a book by a Roman Catholic author in which he stated that the Roman Catholic Church has never taught that the Mass is the re-sacrifice of Jesus Christ. I was amazed because I knew that the statement was simply not true, as even a cursory reading of a Roman Catholic catechism will make clear.

Both these incidents underscored for me the fact that there is great confusion today with respect to the official teachings of the Roman Catholic Church. It seems that, as a general rule, few Roman Catholics know what they believe or what their Church officially teaches. I should add that, in my own experience, there is a similar lack of knowledge of Roman Catholic teaching among Protestants.

I have, therefore, written this book with two very specific purposes in mind: I have sought, firstly, to document the official and authoritative teachings of the Roman Catholic Church on salvation, and thus help to deal with the confusion of beliefs that is so prevalent among both Protestants and Roman Catholics.

In order to document these official teachings, I have employed four authoritative sources: *The Canons and Decrees of the Council of Trent*, *The Documents of Vatican II*, *The Code of Canon Law*, and *The Question and Answer Catholic Catechism*. These documents span the time frame between 1546 and 1981. They show very clearly that the Roman Catholic Church has not changed its teaching with respect to salvation or the major doctrines of the Mass, the Priesthood, Confession and Penance, the Eucharist, or Baptism. These documents underline the consistency of the Church's stand throughout the centuries on each of these major doctrines. I have provided details of these sources in Appendix A. Each one has the official authorization of the Vatican. In order to provide a thorough presentation of what the Roman Catholic Church teaches about these doctrines, I have also included several appendices at the end of the book which give quotations from these documents with respect to the specific doctrinal issues discussed. This should indicate that these quotations have not been taken out of context.

My second objective in writing this book is to compare the teaching of the Roman Catholic Church in a systematic and logical way with the teaching of the Bible, the Word of God, on the specific issues of the Mass, the Priesthood, Confession and Penance, the Eucharist, Baptism, and salvation in general. By this comparison, I hope to set forth, in a positive manner, the teaching of the Bible on the nature of salvation: what it is, how it is accomplished, how it is appropriated, and what it produces.

PART ONE

Roman Catholicism and the Gospel

1: *Tradition and the Word of God*

AUTHORITATIVE STATEMENTS OF ROMAN CATHOLIC TEACHING ON TRADITION AND THE WORD OF GOD[1]

The Documents of Vatican II

Hence there exist a close connection and communication between sacred tradition and sacred Scripture. For both of them, flowing from the same divine wellspring, in a certain way merge into a unity and tend toward the same end. For sacred Scripture is the word of God inasmuch as it is consigned to writing under the inspiration of the divine Spirit. To the successors of the apostles, sacred tradition hands on in its full purity God's word, which was entrusted to the apostles by Christ the Lord and the Holy Spirit . . . Consequently, it is not from sacred Scripture alone that the Church draws her certainty about everything which has been revealed. Therefore both sacred tradition and sacred Scripture are to be accepted and venerated with the same sense of devotion and reverence. Sacred tradition and sacred Scripture form one sacred deposit of the word of God, which is committed to the Church (p. 117).

The Question and Answer Catholic Catechism

59. Where do we find the truths revealed by God?

We find the truths revealed by God in Sacred Scripture and Sacred Tradition.

60. How does Sacred Scripture compare with Sacred Tradition?

[1]A list of authoritative sources employed will be found in Appendix A, pp. 133ff.

Both Sacred Scripture and Sacred Tradition are the inspired word of God, and both are forms of divine revelation. Sacred Scripture is divinely inspired writing, whereas Sacred Tradition is the unwritten word of inspired persons.

89. Why is Sacred Tradition of equal authority with the Bible?

The Bible and Sacred Tradition are of equal authority because they are equally the word of God; both derive from the inspired vision of the ancient prophets, and especially from the infinite wisdom of God incarnate who gave to the apostles what he came down on earth to teach, through them, to all of mankind.

TRADITION AND THE WORD OF GOD – SUMMARY OF NEW TESTAMENT TEACHING

The first issue to be addressed in any discussion of spiritual truth is that of authority. To say something is true or false implies an authoritative standard by which we can make such a judgment. But is there such an authoritative standard by which we can judge whether a particular teaching or system is true or false? The answer is an unequivocal 'yes'. That authoritative standard is the Word of God, the Bible. Jesus Christ himself said of the Bible, 'Thy word is truth' (*Jn. 17:17*). In settling issues of spiritual controversy the Lord Jesus always appealed to the Word of God as an authoritative standard by which to judge truth and falsehood.

Mark's Gospel records an incident in which certain Sadducees came to Jesus to question him. The Sadducees were the religious liberals of Jesus' day and they rejected many of the teachings espoused by the more orthodox sect of the Pharisees. They did not believe in angels or in the resurrection of the dead. A number of these men came to Jesus to ask him a trick question about life after death. Jesus demolished their trick question but went on to say this:

> Is this not the reason you are mistaken, that you do not understand the Scriptures, or the power of God? . . . But regarding the fact that the dead rise again, have you not read in the book of Moses, in the passage about the burning bush, how God spoke to him, saying, 'I am the God of Abraham, and the God of Isaac, and the God of Jacob'? He is not the God of the dead, but of the living; you are greatly mistaken (*Mk. 12:24,25–27*).[2]

Twice in this passage Christ tells these men they are greatly mistaken in their views. The reason is that they do not understand the Scriptures. He appeals to those Scriptures to correct the false concepts these men held. He points to the Word of God as an authoritative standard by which to judge truth and error. These men are greatly mistaken because the views they hold and the doctrines they teach contradict the Word of God.

Here you have two opposing views of truth. One says there is no resurrection from the dead, the other says there is. How do you determine which is true? You go to the Word of God. The Lord Jesus Christ is the Son of God. He is God in human flesh and therefore whatever he teaches is absolute truth. And according to him the Word of God is the final and authoritative standard by which all claims to truth are to be judged.

This principle obviously has a direct bearing upon the whole issue of tradition. The Roman Catholic Church teaches that tradition as well as the Bible constitutes the revealed Word of God. It teaches that the teaching of the Church Fathers, the Church Councils, and the Traditions of the Church are all 'one sacred deposit of the Word of God'.

John Hardon S.J. makes the following statements in his *Question and Answer Catholic Catechism*:

[2]Scripture references are from the *New American Standard Bible*, The Lockman Foundation, 1963.

Sacred Tradition is the unwritten word of God that the prophets and apostles received through the inspiration of the Holy Spirit and, under His guidance, the Church has handed on to the Christian world.

Both Sacred Scripture and Sacred Tradition are the inspired word of God, and both are forms of divine revelation. Sacred Scripture is divinely inspired writing, whereas Sacred Tradition is the unwritten word of inspired persons.

Jesus Christ had some interesting things to say about tradition:

> Then some Pharisees and scribes came to Jesus from Jerusalem, saying, 'Why do Your disciples transgress the tradition of the elders? For they do not wash their hands when they eat bread.' And He answered and said to them, 'And why do you yourselves transgress the commandment of God for the sake of your tradition? For God said, "Honor your father and mother" . . . But you say, "Whoever shall say to his father or mother, 'Anything of mine you might have been helped by has been given to God,' he is not to honor his father or his mother." And thus *you invalidated the word of God for the sake of your tradition*. You hypocrites, rightly did Isaiah prophesy of you, saying, "This people honors Me with their lips, but their heart is far away from Me. But in vain do they worship Me, teaching as doctrines the precepts of men"' (*Matt. 15:1–9*).

In a parallel passage in Mark 7:5–13 much of the same teaching by Jesus is recorded. The Pharisees ask why the disciples do not walk according to *the tradition of the elders*. In response Jesus denounces the scribes and Pharisees and their observance of tradition which is in violation of the Word of God. In effect they have elevated the teachings of men above the Scriptures. The following sums up Jesus' evaluation:

1. You teach as doctrines the precepts of men.
2. Neglecting the commandment of God you hold to the tradition of men.
3. You set aside the commandment of God in order to keep your tradition.
4. You invalidate the Word of God by your tradition which you have handed down.

We should note that Jesus is not condemning tradition simply because it is tradition. All tradition is not wrong. What he is condemning is the elevating of tradition or the teaching of men to equality with the Word of God. He condemned the scribes and Pharisees for following tradition which violated and invalidated the Word of God. And then he rebuked them for so teaching others.

Tradition is not necessarily wrong, but tradition is not the Word of God, and for tradition to be acceptable to God, it must never contradict or violate the clear teaching of the Bible. All tradition must be judged by the truth of Scripture, including traditions which have their original roots in Scripture. The traditions that the scribes and Pharisees adhered to, but which Jesus denounced, were traditions which had their roots in mistaken interpretations of the Bible.

There is one obvious and definitive test which we can apply to all teaching and tradition to determine if it is true. That test is this: if the tradition or the teaching, even though it arises from the interpretation of a passage of Scripture, contradicts the clear teaching of another portion of Scripture, then that particular tradition or teaching is incorrect, for Scripture never contradicts Scripture.

The Word of God alone is our final authority, never tradition. We are told in 2 Timothy 3:16,17 that 'All Scripture is inspired by God and profitable for teaching, for reproof, for correction, for training in righteousness; that the man of God may be adequate, equipped for every good work.' All Scripture is inspired and is therefore authoritative. And because it is inspired, that is, because it is the Word of a self-consistent God, it will never contradict itself.

Consequently, we can judge whether or not a particular teaching or tradition is true by comparing it to the Word of God. If it is consistent with the Word of God, then we can accept it as truth. However, if it clearly contradicts the teaching of the Bible or makes the Word of God contradict itself, then we know that it is error, and is to be rejected. Otherwise we shall fall into the same condemnation which Jesus uttered against the Pharisees.

One question this whole issue brings up is this: can the true church of God fall into error? The answer to that question, based upon the history of God's people in the Bible is 'yes'. It is possible for the church leadership to fall into error and be led astray from the truth. For example, the apostle Peter was publicly rebuked by Paul for the hypocrisy of which he was guilty (*Gal. 2:11–14*).

On an earlier occasion the apostle Peter was rebuked by Christ because he tried to hinder the Lord from going to the cross. 'But He turned and said to Peter, "Get behind Me, Satan! You are a stumbling-block to Me; for you are not setting your mind on God's interests, but man's"' (*Matt. 16:23*). The Lord Jesus actually addressed *Peter* as Satan, for Satan was using Peter to try to divert him from the will of God. This all transpired after Peter had been told that he was to be given the keys of the kingdom of heaven (*Matt. 16:18–19*).

Of course, the example of God's chosen people, the Jews, during the time of the Lord Jesus himself, shows us clearly that it is possible for the church's leadership to be deceived. Jesus' words about tradition were spoken against the scribes and Pharisees, the religious leadership of God's chosen people and the true church of that day. They had fallen into error and had become so blind that they failed to recognise

Jesus as the Messiah. They fell into the error of misinterpreting the Word of God and of elevating tradition and the teachings of the elders to a level equal in authority to the Scriptures, even though those teachings contradicted the Word of God. In addition to this Jesus claimed that the religious leadership of his day, because of their adherence to tradition and misinterpretation of Scripture, were actually responsible for hindering people from entering the kingdom of God: 'Woe to you lawyers! For you have taken away the key of knowledge; you did not enter in yourselves, and those who were entering in you hindered' (*Lk. 11:52*). 'But woe to you, scribes and Pharisees, hypocrites, because you shut off the kingdom of heaven from men; for you do not enter in yourselves, nor do you allow those who are entering to go in' (*Matt. 23:13*). If this was true of the religious leadership of God's chosen people in the day of Jesus Christ, there is absolutely no guarantee that a church leadership will not fall into error and mislead people.

Were the Pharisees and scribes of Jesus' day intentionally trying to deceive people? Not necessarily! Many of them were doing what they sincerely felt was right. But they were wrong and consequently they were deceiving people and leading them astray. Sincerity is no guarantee against error. A man can be sincerely wrong. In the final analysis, as Christ taught, the Word of God is the final authority for determining what is truth and what is error. Any teaching which contradicts the Word of God must be rejected: 'To the law and to the testimony: if they speak not according to this word, it is because there is no light in them' (*Is. 8:20, A.V.*).

Luke records that when Paul came to Berea, and preached the gospel in the local Jewish synagogue, the Bereans 'were more noble-minded than those in Thessalonica, for they received the word with great eagerness, *examining the Scriptures daily*, to see whether these things were so' (*Acts 17:11*). The Bereans compared Paul's doctrines with the

Word of God to see if his teachings were consistent with the teachings of the Word of God. Only then would they accept the gospel he was preaching. They knew that any teaching that truly originates from God would not contradict what he had already revealed in his Word.

It is in this spirit that we shall examine the teachings of the Roman Catholic Church.

2: *The Mass*

AUTHORITATIVE STATEMENTS OF ROMAN CATHOLIC TEACHING ON THE MASS[1]

The Council of Trent

Session XXII: On the Sacrifice of the Mass

Canon I. If any one saith, that in the mass a true and proper sacrifice is not offered to God; or, that to be offered is nothing else but that Christ is given us to eat: let him be anathema.

Canon III. If any one saith, that the sacrifice of the mass is only a sacrifice of praise and of thanksgiving; or, that it is a bare commemoration of the sacrifice consummated on the cross, but not a propitiatory sacrifice; or, that it profits him only who receives; and that it ought not to be offered for the living and the dead for sins, pains, satisfactions, and other necessities: let him be anathema.

The Question and Answer Catholic Catechism

1264. How is the Sacrifice of the Cross continued on earth?

The Sacrifice of the Cross is continued on earth through the Sacrifice of the Mass.

1265. What is the Sacrifice of the Mass?

The Sacrifice of the Mass is the true and properly called Sacrifice of the New Law. It is the Sacrifice in which Christ is

[1]A list of authoritative statements of Roman Catholic teaching on the Mass will be found in Appendix B, pp. 136ff.

offered under the species of bread and wine in an unbloody manner. The Sacrifice of the altar, then, is no mere empty commemoration of the Passion and Death of Jesus Christ, but a true and proper act of sacrifice. Christ, the eternal High Priest, in an unbloody way offers himself a most acceptable Victim to the eternal Father, as he did upon the Cross.

1269. How does the Mass re-present Calvary?

The Mass re-presents Calvary by continuing Christ's sacrifice of himself to his heavenly Father. In the Mass, no less than on Calvary, Jesus really offers his life to his heavenly Father. This is possible because in the Mass is the same priest, Jesus Christ, who with his human will (united to the divine) offers himself; and it is the same victim, Jesus Christ, whose human life (united with the divinity) is sacrificed.

1277. Does the Mass detract from the one, unique Sacrifice of the Cross?

The Mass in no way detracts from the one, unique Sacrifice of the Cross because the Mass is the same Sacrifice as that of the Cross, to continue on earth until the end of time. Christ not only was the priest who offered himself to his heavenly Father. He is the priest whose intercession for sinful mankind continues, only now he communicates the graces he had won for us by his bloody Passion and Death. The Mass, therefore, no less than the Cross, is expiatory for sins; but now the expiation is experienced by those for whom, on the Cross, the title of God's mercy had been gained.

1279. How are the merits of Calvary dispensed through the Holy Sacrifice of the Mass?

The merits of Calvary are dispensed through the Mass in that the graces Christ gained for us on the Cross are communicated by the Eucharistic Sacrifice.

SUMMARY OF ROMAN CATHOLIC TEACHING

It is clear from these authoritative sources that in Roman Catholic theology the Mass is far more than a mere memorial.

It is a *sacrifice*. The Roman Catholic Church teaches that the Mass is a continuation of the sacrifice of the Cross and that it is absolutely necessary for salvation. It teaches that the Mass is the same sacrifice as Calvary except that now it is unbloody, and because it is the same sacrifice as that of Calvary, it is expiatory for sins. According to the Church it is through the Mass that Christ communicates the graces he has won for men on the cross. It is the sacrament through which all the benefits of Christ's death are channelled to an individual person.

BIBLICAL TEACHING

How does this teaching compare with the Word of God? Is it consistent with what the Bible teaches about the sacrifice of Christ? We find the answer to that question in the Letter to the Hebrews which gives very clear and detailed teaching on the nature of the sacrifice of the Lord Jesus. (In the following quotations the crucial words have been printed in italics.)

> *Hebrews 7:26–27*: For it was fitting that we should have such a high priest, holy, innocent, undefiled, separated from sinners and exalted above the heavens; *who does not need daily*, like those high priests, to offer up sacrifices, first for His own sins, and then for the sins of the people, because this He did *once for all* when He offered up Himself.
>
> *Hebrews 9:11–12*: But when Christ appeared as a high priest of the good things to come, He entered through the greater and more perfect tabernacle, not made with hands, that is to say, not of this creation; and not through the blood of goats and calves, but through His own blood, He entered the holy place *once for all*, having obtained eternal redemption.
>
> *Hebrews 9:24–26,28*: For Christ did not enter a holy place made with hands, a mere copy of the true one, but into heaven itself, now to appear in the presence of God for us; *nor was it that He should offer Himself often*, as the high priest

> enters the holy place year by year with blood not his own. *Otherwise, He would have needed to suffer often* since the foundation of the world; but now *once* at the consummation of the ages He has been manifested to *put away sin* by the sacrifice of Himself . . . So Christ also, having been offered *once* to bear the sins of many, shall *appear* a second time for salvation without reference to sin, to those who eagerly await Him.
>
> *Hebrews 10:10–14,18*: By this will we have been sanctified through the offering of the body of Jesus Christ *once for all*. And every priest stands daily ministering and offering time after time the same sacrifices, which can never take away sins; but He, having offered *one sacrifice for sins for all time*, sat down at the right hand of God, waiting from that time onward until His enemies be made a footstool for His feet. For by *one offering* He has *perfected for all time* those who are sanctified . . . Now where there is forgiveness of these things, *there is no longer any offering for sin*.

Paul's emphasis in his Letter to the Romans is similar:

> *Romans 6:9–10*: Knowing that *Christ*, having been raised from the dead, *is never to die again*; death no longer is master over Him. For *the death that He died, He died to sin, once for all*; but the life that He lives, He lives to God.

SUMMARY OF THE BIBLICAL TEACHING

In these passages the sacrifice of Jesus is contrasted with the old Jewish sacrificial system: 'And every priest stands daily ministering . . . *but He*, having offered one sacrifice for sins for all time . . .' (*Heb. 10:11–12*).

In that old system the priests had to offer sacrifices continually over and over again because the blood of bulls and goats could never take away sins but only cover them

('For it is impossible for the blood of bulls and goats to take away sins', *Heb. 10:4*). However, with the coming of Christ and his sacrifice the old sacrificial system has been completely done away with, because the blood of Jesus Christ *takes away* sin. Through his blood there is complete forgiveness ('but now once at the consummation of the ages He has been manifested to *put away* sin by the sacrifice of Himself', *Heb. 9:26*).

The passages quoted teach that the sacrifice of Christ is a *once for all* sacrifice that is *never to be repeated*. Seven times in the passages quoted it is emphasised that the sacrifice was *once* for all. It cannot be repeated, for Jesus can never die again (*Rom. 6:9–10*). His one sacrifice is complete. No further sacrifice needs to be accomplished: 'Now where there is forgiveness of these things, there is no longer any offering for sin' (*Heb. 10:18*). This means that all sacrifices for sin have come to an end.

There is an obvious contradiction here between the teaching of the Roman Catholic Church and the teaching of the Scriptures. The Roman Catholic Church teaches that Christ's sacrifice must be repeated again and again: that his one offering is not sufficient to cleanse from all sin but that repeated sacrifices in the Mass are necessary for salvation.

To see clearly the contrast between the Bible and the teaching of the Roman Catholic Church with respect to the sacrifice of Jesus, note the following chart:

THE BIBLE	ROMAN CATHOLIC TEACHING
1. One sacrifice for sins for all time: one sacrifice non-repeatable (*Heb. 7:24, 9:12, 9:22–29, 10:12,14*).	1. Re-sacrifice of Jesus daily/often repeated.

2. He is never to die again, having died once (*Rom. 6:9–10*).	2. Jesus dies often.
3. Without the shedding of blood there is no forgiveness of sins (*Heb. 9:22*).	3. Unbloody sacrifice which forgives the guilt of sin.
4. Sins are taken away and completely dealt with in the one sacrifice of Jesus (*Heb. 10:10,14, 18; 9:26*).	4. Sins must continually be atoned for in the Mass. Sin has not been put away with the one sacrifice of Jesus.
5. For by one offering He has perfected for all time those who are sanctified (*Heb. 10:14*).	5. The one sacrifice for sins is not a sufficient payment to God for forgiveness.
6. Since there is forgiveness for these things there is no longer any offering for sins (*Heb. 10:18*).	6. Many offerings needed. The sacrifices must be continued.

The Lord Jesus Christ could not have instituted the Mass. On the contrary, Scripture tells us that all sacrifices have now ceased with his one perfect and complete sacrifice.

> The celebration of the mass is the chief duty of the Roman priesthood. Yet the New Testament gives no instruction as to how to offer mass, and in fact there is not so much as one line on the subject in Scripture. Christ sent the apostles to teach and to baptize, not to say mass . . . Paul gave many instructions and exhortations concerning the government and duties of the churches, but he says nothing about the sacrifice of the mass . . . The writer of the Epistle to the Hebrews has much to say about the endless repetition and futility of the ancient sacrifices. He shows that their only value was to symbolize and point forward to the one true sacrifice that was to be made by Christ . . . (10:10–14).

> The New Testament, therefore, announces the termination of all sacrifices, declaring that Christ alone is our true sacrifice, and that He offered Himself 'once for all,' thus forever ending all other sacrifices (Loraine Boettner, *Roman Catholicism*, 1962, pp. 171–72).

As we have already pointed out, there is a basic principle of biblical interpretation which must be carefully observed. Because the Bible is the Word of God we know that it cannot contradict itself. The Word of God is truth (*Jn. 17:17*). Therefore, if our interpretation of a particular passage of Scripture causes that passage to contradict the clear teaching of another passage, our interpretation is incorrect.

The Letter to the Hebrews states over and over again that the sacrifice of Jesus was once for all and therefore cannot be repeated. For the Roman Catholic Church to interpret other Scriptures, such as the passages on the Last Supper, to mean that Christ was instituting a sacrament for the continuation of his sacrifice is to cause Scripture to contradict itself.

The Bible stands completely opposed to everything the Roman Catholic Church teaches with regard to the Mass. The contradictions are irreconcilable. The Word of God teaches one thing while the Roman Church teaches another.

Furthermore, we do not need a Mass for the forgiveness of sins. Jesus' *one* sacrifice is complete and sufficient. All who come to him to receive him as Saviour *by faith*, and submit to him as Lord will find complete forgiveness for all sins on the basis of his one all-sufficient sacrifice on the cross. Our faith is to be in a person and his finished work, not in a Church and its sacraments.

3: *The Priesthood*

AUTHORITATIVE STATEMENTS OF ROMAN CATHOLIC TEACHING ON THE PRIESTHOOD[1]

The Council of Trent

Session XXIII: On the Sacrament of Order

Canon I. If any one saith, that there is not in the New Testament a visible and external priesthood; or, that there is not any power of consecrating and offering the true body and blood of the Lord, and of forgiving and retaining sins, but only an office and bare ministry of preaching the Gospel; or, that those who do not preach are not priests at all: let him be anathema.

Session XXII: On the Sacrifice of the Mass

Canon II. If any one saith, that by those words, Do this for the commemoration of me (*Luke xxii. 19*), *Christ did not institute the apostles priests; or, did not ordain that they and other priests should offer his own body and blood: let him be anathema.*

The Question and Answer Catholic Catechism

1466. When did Christ institute the sacrament of orders?

Christ actually instituted the sacrament of orders at the Last Supper. After he had consecrated the bread and wine, and

[1] A list of authoritative statements of Roman Catholic teaching on the Priesthood will be found in Appendix C, pp. 142ff.

changed them into his own body and blood, he told the apostles to 'do this as a memorial of me' (Luke 22:19). By this he was conferring on the apostles and their successors the principal power of this sacrament, namely to consecrate and offer his body and blood in the Sacrifice of the Mass.

1488. What is the primary ministry of a priest?

The primary ministry of a priest is to consecrate and offer the Holy Eucharist, and to forgive sins. In this, priests differ from deacons who do not receive the power to consecrate the Eucharist, offer Mass, or forgive sins by sacramental absolution.

SUMMARY OF ROMAN CATHOLIC TEACHING

It is evident from these authoritative sources that the Roman Catholic Church teaches that the Lord Jesus Christ personally instituted the office of priesthood for the exercise of two primary responsibilities: the first is to offer the sacrifice of the Mass and the second is to hear confession of sins and to make absolution. Thus in the exercise of his responsibilities, specifically in the sacrifice of the Mass and through confession and penance, the priest is a mediator.

The Greek word for mediator in the New Testament is the word *mesitēs*, that is, 'one who intervenes between two, either in order to make or restore peace and friendship; a medium of communication, an arbitrator' (Thayer's *Greek–English Lexicon of the New Testament*, 1887). Thus a mediator is one who goes between two individuals or parties in order to reconcile the one with the other.

Does the Bible teach that the Lord Jesus Christ instituted a special class of men in the church known as priests who would be given the authority to reconcile men with God through the Mass and through confession and penance? The answer to that question, as we shall see, is quite simply 'no'.

First of all, as we noted in the previous chapter, the whole concept of continuing sacrifices is completely contradictory to the teaching of the Word of God. The Lord Jesus did not commission or institute a human priesthood, beginning with the apostles, who would continue the offering of sacrifices in a Mass. All sacrifices have now been abolished because the 'once for all' sacrifice of Jesus Christ is complete. Since the sacrifices have been abolished (*Heb. 10*) there is no longer any need for a priesthood. Whatever it was the Lord Jesus was commissioning his apostles to do, it was not to authorise them to become priests who would continue his sacrifice in the offering of a Mass.

Some contemporary Roman Catholic writers emphasise that the priest does not actually re-present Christ's sacrifice as a literal sacrifice, but only re-presents his one-time historical sacrifice as a memorial. One such writer has written:

> The Catholic Church has never taught that in the Mass Jesus is 're-sacrificed' or offered up to suffer again. The Catholic Mass is called a sacrifice because it 're-presents,' 're-enacts,' or presents once again before us, the one sacrifice of Christ on Calvary. Jesus Christ was sacrificed once, but God, in his mercy, makes present to us once again the one sacrifice of Christ through the Mass so that we human beings can enter more deeply into the reality and significance of that sacrifice. Catholics believe that this is possible because Jesus Christ is 'the same yesterday, today and forever' (Heb. 13:8). What Jesus did in the *past* – his death on the cross – is *present* to God. God can make this sacrifice present to us when Christians gather to celebrate the Lord's Supper or Eucharist in his memory. Therefore, Catholic Christians believe that Jesus is not 're-sacrificed' in the Mass, but that his one sacrifice on Calvary is made real and present to us by God, so that we can enter into this central mystery of our faith in a new way (Alan Schreck, *Catholic and Christian*, 1984, pp. 133–34).

Schreck's statements are a complete denial of what the Roman Catholic Church *authoritatively* teaches with respect to the Mass and the Priesthood. He says that the Church has never taught that the Mass is the re-sacrifice of Jesus Christ. But this is simply not true. The Council of Trent says that it is a true sacrifice, which is propitiatory for sin, and it calls down an anathema on anyone who denies this.[2] John Hardon S.J. says,

> The Sacrifice of the Cross is continued on earth through the Sacrifice of the Mass . . . It is the Sacrifice in which Christ is offered under the species of bread and wine in an unbloody manner. The Sacrifice of the altar, then, is no mere empty commemoration of the Passion and Death of Jesus Christ, but a true and proper act of sacrifice . . . The Mass re-presents Christ's sacrifice of himself to his heavenly Father. In the Mass, no less than on Calvary, Jesus really offers his life to his heavenly Father . . . The Mass in no way detracts from the one, unique Sacrifice of the Cross because the Mass is the same sacrifice as that of the Cross, to continue on earth until the end of time . . . The Mass, therefore, no less than the Cross, is expiatory for sins . . .' (*The Question and Answer Catholic Catechism*, 1264, 1265, 1269, 1277).

The official teachings of the Roman Catholic Church are clear. The priest does not merely commemorate the death and sacrifice of Christ, but actually continues his sacrifice through the sacrifice of the Mass. But such teaching flatly contradicts the teaching we have seen in Hebrews chapters 7 and 10. Since the Bible is the Word of God and cannot contradict itself, the interpretation of the Roman Catholic Church must be incorrect.

It will be helpful here to look closely at what the Bible actually teaches about the priesthood.

In the Old Testament dispensation God appointed the tribe of Levi to the priesthood. They had the responsibility of

[2]See Canons at the beginning of this chapter, and Appendix C, pp. 142ff.

representing the people before God and acting as mediators between God and the people. That is the essential idea of a priest; he is one who mediates between God and man. God appointed these mediators because, in their sinful state, men could not come before him or have fellowship with him without their mediation in offering sacrifices. The central responsibility of the priest in the Old Testament dispensation was to minister in the sanctuary before God, offering sacrifices to him on behalf of the people and to teach them the law of God: 'For every high priest taken from among men is appointed on behalf of men in things pertaining to God, in order to offer both gifts and sacrifices for sins' (*Heb. 5:1*).

The entire sacrificial system in the Old Testament foreshadowed the one great sacrifice of Jesus as the Lamb of God who takes away the sins of the world. It has therefore been completely abolished. Similarly the priesthood which God established in the Old Testament was a foreshadowing of that which would one day be fulfilled in our Great High Priest the Lord Jesus Christ. 'With the coming of Christ . . . and with the accomplishment of His work of redemption, each of these offices, as it functioned on the human level, reached its fulfillment and was abolished' (Loraine Boettner, *Roman Catholicism*, p. 44).

Hebrews 7:11–24 makes very clear that the human priesthood of the Old Testament has been done away with. It has been replaced by the priesthood of Jesus Christ and he is now a priest for ever. The old covenant's priesthood and sacrifices have become obsolete (*Heb. 8:13*) and have been set aside.

The key biblical authority for this teaching is Hebrews 7:12, 7:18–19, and 7:24:

> For when the *priesthood* is *changed*, of necessity there takes place a change of law also (*Heb. 7:12*).

> For, on the one hand, there is a *setting aside* of a former commandment because of its weakness and uselessness

(for the Law made nothing perfect), and on the other hand there is a bringing in of a better hope, through which we draw near to God (*Heb.* 7:18–19).

But He, on the other hand, because He *abides forever*, holds His priesthood *permanently* (*Heb.* 7:24).

These verses tell us that the Aaronic priesthood was changed with the coming of Christ. A new priesthood, one according to the order of Melchizedek, was inaugurated. There is a *setting aside* of a former commandment (the Old Testament dispensation of sacrifice and human priesthood which could not bring in perfection) and now, that which is perfect has come. What the Old Testament priesthood could not do, Jesus Christ has done. Consequently the old system is set aside. The Greek word translated 'setting aside' is *athetēsis*. It implies abolition. Thus the Old Testament priesthood has been abolished. 'The declaration, "Thou art a priest forever after the order of Melchizedek," thus announces the *abrogation* of the earlier law which instituted the Aaronic order' (F. F. Bruce, *Hebrews*, 1964, p. 148).

The old system, the old human priesthood, has been set aside and replaced by the eternal priesthood of Jesus Christ. Because he abides for ever, he holds his priesthood *permanently* (*Heb.* 7:24). The word 'permanently' is the Greek word *aparabatos* which means 'unchangeable, not liable to pass to a successor' (*Thayer's Greek–English Lexicon*).

Jesus Christ could not have instituted a human priesthood through the disciples, for the Bible teaches that he exercises an exclusive priesthood for ever. It cannot be shared by or transferred to anyone else. The Mosaic system in the Old Testament foreshadowed the person and work of the Lord Jesus Christ. Now that he has come, the old system has been completely abolished.

In accordance with this New Testament change in the priesthood, through which the old order of ritual and

> sacrifice which prefigured the atoning work of Christ has been fulfilled and Christ alone has become our true High Priest, the human priesthood as a distinct and separate order of men has fulfilled its function and has been abolished (Loraine Boettner, *Roman Catholicism*, p. 44).

The entire Letter to the Hebrews was written to instruct and warn Jewish Christians who had come out of Judaism, but who, because of persecution, were being tempted to renounce Christianity and to return to the old Mosaic system. The Letter shows that the entire Mosaic system has now been set aside by God because Jesus Christ is the perfect fulfilment of all that the old system signified. Now men have direct access to God through Jesus Christ and they no longer need a human system of sacrifices and priests. Men can now come directly to God through Jesus Christ. *He* has become our sacrifice. *He* has become our priest, and *he* is the only mediator between ourselves and God.

God did not intend the Mosaic system to be permanent. It was merely a temporary arrangement to teach men that they must come to him through a priest, and by means of a sacrificial death. But when the Son of God came, as the perfect fulfilment of all that the old system signified, the old covenant and its sacrificial system were set aside and a new covenant and a perfect means of coming to God took its place. Thus 'there is one God, and one mediator also between God and men, the man Christ Jesus' (*1 Tim. 2:5*). Christ himself said, '*I* am the way, and the truth, and the life; no one comes to the Father, but through *Me*' (*Jn. 14:6*).

Jesus Christ is now the only priest God recognises; he is the only priest men need because his work of sacrifice for sin is perfect. He now stands continually before God for his people. He alone can reconcile man with God, and we have now been given the right of access to God *directly* through him: 'For *through Him* we both have our access in one Spirit to the Father' (*Eph. 2:18*).

In fact, in the entire New Testament, no mention is made of a new order of priests with the authority to continue sacrifices and forgive sins and thereby act as mediators between God and man.

The writers of the New Testament had two separate words for *elder* and *priest*. They do not mean the same thing at all, and the New Testament never confuses them. It never says *presbuteros*, elder, when it means *priest*. The New Testament word for priest is *hiereus*. In Greek, from Homer down, this word had a singular meaning. It meant a man appointed, or consecrated, or otherwise endowed with power to perform certain technical functions of ritual worship, especially to offer acceptable sacrifices, and to make effectual prayers. Likewise in the Septuagint, *hiereus* is the regular if not invariable translation of the Old Testament *kohen* and *kahen*, the only Hebrew word for priest. It occurs more than 400 times in the Old Testament in this sense. In the New Testament *hiereus* always means priest, never means elder. There is not anywhere in the New Testament the shadow of an allusion to a Christian priest in the ordinary sense of the word, that is, a man qualified as over against others not qualified for the special function of offering sacrifices, making priestly intercessions, or performing any other act which only a priest can perform. The Epistle to the Hebrews attributed both priesthood and high-priesthood to Christ and to Him alone. The argument of the Epistle not only indicates that a Christian priesthood was unknown to the writer, but that such a priesthood is unallowable. It is to Jesus only that Christians look as to a priest. He has performed perfectly and permanently the function of a priest for all believers. His priesthood, being perfect and eternal, renders a continuous human priesthood both needless and anachronistic (*Chicago Lutheran Theological Seminary Record*, July 1952, cited Boettner, p. 47).

In several places Paul lists the different kinds of ministries and men who are specifically set apart and gifted by God to do a work within the church, such as apostles, prophets, evangelists, pastors and teachers (*Eph. 4:11, 1 Cor. 12:28*). Nowhere does Paul mention priests. Paul did appoint elders in the churches, but, as we have seen, 'priest' is a different word altogether.

In contradistinction to a select class of men set apart for the special ministry of priesthood, the New Testament teaches that *all* Christians are priests. But the only sacrifices they offer are spiritual in that they have access to the throne of God in prayer and can plead before him on behalf of men:

> But you are a chosen race, a royal *priesthood*, a holy nation, a people for God's own possession, that you may proclaim the excellencies of Him who has called you out of darkness into His marvelous light (*1 Pet. 2:9*).

> To Him who loves us, and released us from our sins by His blood, and He has made us to be a kingdom, *priests* to His God and Father' (*Rev. 1:5–6*).

> Under the New Testament economy, there is but one priest, in the strict meaning of that word as defined by the Apostle Paul: 'One taken from among men, ordained for men in things pertaining to God, that he may offer both gifts and sacrifices for sins' (*Heb. 5:1*). Our great High Priest, of whom all the priests under the Mosaic dispensation were but figures, is 'the one Mediator between God and man' (*1 Tim. 2:5*). He presents the only effectual atoning sacrifice. He, on the ground of that sacrifice, makes intercession for those who come to God through him, and obtains acceptance both for them and their services, and authoritatively blesses his people . . .
>
> It is common enough, however, in the New Testament, to represent all Christians as figurative priests, in the sense of persons solemnly consecrated to and habitually engaged in the divine service. These two views are given us in the passage before us. Ye are 'a holy priesthood,' and ye are a

priesthood engaged in presenting to God 'spiritual sacrifices, which are acceptable to God by Christ Jesus . . .'

Christians are a 'holy,' a consecrated priesthood. You are aware that the priests under the Old Testament were separated from among their brethren. They were so by their birth, and by their consecration. As sons of Aaron, they belonged to the priestly order. In like manner, all Christians, by their being born again, are set apart to the service of God. And as Aaron's sons were consecrated by the sprinkling of blood and the washing of water; so Christians have their conscience sprinkled by the blood of Him, 'who, by the eternal Spirit, offered himself a sacrifice to God without spot,' and are purified 'by the washing of regeneration, and the renewing of the Holy Ghost' (*Heb. 9:14; Tit. 3:5*).

As they resemble the priests in their consecration, so they resemble them also in their work. They 'offer up spiritual sacrifices.' . . . The leading idea is, that Christians are brought into a very near relation to God; and that the whole of their lives should be devoted to his spiritual service. They are to 'offer the sacrifice of praise to God continually, that is, the fruit of the lips,' . . . 'giving thanks to his name.' 'To do good and communicate they are not to forget, for with such sacrifices God is well pleased.' They are to 'present their bodies' – themselves, embodied living beings, not the dead bodies of slain beasts – 'a living sacrifice.' 'Whether they eat, or drink, or whatsoever they do, they are to do all to the glory of God;' and 'whatsoever they do in word or in deed, they are to do it in the name of the Lord Jesus, giving thanks to God the Father by him' (John Brown, *Expository Discourses on 1 Peter*, Volume 1, 1975 reprint, pp. 249–52).

1 Peter 2:5,9 refers to a priesthood that *all* believers in Jesus share. We are a kingdom of priests. But this priesthood has nothing to do with sacrifices for sin, nor with men coming to God through our mediation. Men are to go directly to God through Jesus Christ, completely bypassing any human

agency. We have no need of a human priesthood when we have the divine priest, Jesus Christ, to whom we can go at any time because he has made the perfect sacrifice. He alone is the mediator between ourselves and God. There is, and can be, no other (*1 Tim. 2:5*).

Roman Catholic teaching on the priesthood is therefore in direct contradiction to the teaching of the Word of God. God no longer authorises a human priesthood with its sacrifices to mediate between himself and man.

But what about the Roman Catholic teaching that men need a human priest to absolve them from sin by means of confession and penance? We will look at that question in detail in our next chapter.

4: *Confession and Penance*

AUTHORITATIVE STATEMENTS OF ROMAN CATHOLIC TEACHING ON CONFESSION AND PENANCE[1]

The Council of Trent

Session XIV: On the Most Holy Sacraments of Penance and Extreme Unction

Chapter VI: On the Ministry of this sacrament, and on Absolution

But although the absolution of the priest is the dispensation of another's bounty, yet is it not a bare ministry only, whether of announcing the Gospel, or of declaring that sins are forgiven, but is after the manner of a judicial act, whereby sentence is pronounced by the priest as by a judge.

On the Most Holy Sacrament of Penance

Canon VI. If any one denieth, either that sacramental confession was instituted, or is necessary to salvation, of divine right; or saith, that the manner of confessing secretly to a priest alone, which the Church hath ever observed from the beginning, and doth observe, is alien from the institution and command of Christ, and is a human invention: let him be anathema.

Canon IX. If any one saith, that the sacramental absolution of the priest is not a judicial act, but a bare ministry of pronouncing

[1]A list of authoritative statements of Roman Catholic teaching on Confession and Penance will be found in Appendix D, pp. 146ff.

and declaring sins to be forgiven to him who confesses; provided only he believe himself to be absolved, or [even though] the priest absolve not in earnest, but in joke; or saith, that the confession of the penitent is not required, in order that the priest may be able to absolve him: let him be anathema.

The Question and Answer Catholic Catechism

1320. Why is the virtue of penance necessary?

The virtue of penance is necessary for a sinner to be reconciled with God. If we expect his forgiveness, we must repent. Penance is also necessary because we must expiate and make reparation for the punishment which is due for our sins. That is why Christ tells us, 'Unless you repent you will all perish' (Luke 13:5).

1321. What is the sacrament of penance?

Penance is the sacrament instituted by Christ in which sinners are reconciled with God through the absolution of the priest.

1326. What is the matter and form of the sacrament of penance?

The form of the sacrament is the words of absolution, which are said orally by an authorized priest. Essential for absolution are the words, 'I absolve you from your sins.' The matter of the sacrament is the required acts of the penitent, namely, contrition, confession, and satisfaction.

1389. How is satisfaction expiatory?

Satisfaction is expiatory by making up for the failure in love of God which is the root cause of sin, by voluntarily suffering to make up for self-indulgence, and by enduring pain in reparation for the harm or disorder caused by the commission of sin.

1395. What is extra-sacramental satisfaction?

Extra-sacramental satisfaction is every form of expiation offered to God outside the sacrament of penance. Our works of satisfaction are meritorious if they are done while in the state of grace and in a spirit of penance.

1400. How can we make up for sin?

We can make up for sin through the sorrows and trials of life, including the pain of death, or through the purifying penalties in the life beyond. Sin can also be expiated through indulgences.

SUMMARY OF ROMAN CATHOLIC TEACHING

The Roman Catholic Church teaches that through the apostles the Lord Jesus Christ established a human priesthood with divine authority to forgive sins and to absolve men from guilt and bring them into a state of forgiveness and reconciliation with God.

The Roman Catholic Church teaches that this is no mere formality, but that the priest stands in the place of God as judge and performs a judicial act. It further teaches that, apart from confessing sins to an authorised priest and doing the penance required, there can be no forgiveness of sins. Confession and penance are therefore seen as necessary for salvation. The Roman Church further teaches that by good works, prayers, fastings, participation in the sacraments, indulgences, the enduring of suffering and by acts of charity, an individual can atone for his guilt, merit God's grace, and remove the temporal punishment his sin deserves. In other words, an individual can make satisfaction for his own sins through his own works.

The following verses are the major biblical texts which the Roman Catholic Church uses as the basis for its teaching on confession and penance.

> *Matthew 16:16–19*: Then Simon Peter spoke up, 'You are the Christ,' he said 'The Son of the Living God'. Jesus replied . . . 'you are a happy man! Because it was not flesh and blood that revealed this to you but my Father in heaven. So I now say to you: You are Peter and on this rock I will build my Church. And the gates of the underworld can never hold out against it. I will give you the keys of the kingdom of heaven: whatever you bind on earth shall be considered bound in heaven; whatever you loose on earth shall be considered loosed in heaven' (*Jerusalem Bible*).

John 20:23: If you forgive the sins of any, their sins have been forgiven them; if you retain the sins of any, they have been retained.

WHAT THE BIBLE TEACHES

The questions we must ask are: Do these verses actually teach the Roman Catholic doctrine of confession and penance? Is such an interpretation of these verses consistent with the teaching of the rest of the Bible?

Clearly, the answer to our questions must be negative. These verses do *not* teach that a priest has the authority to forgive sins. Rome's interpretation of these verses is not consistent with the teaching of the rest of the Bible. Indeed, it causes the Bible to contradict itself. This is true for the following reasons:

We have already seen in our studies on the Mass and the Priesthood that Christ did not institute a special group of men as priests to continue the offering of sacrifices until he returns. On the contrary, all human priesthood has been abolished and replaced by the priesthood of Jesus Christ. Since there is no longer a priesthood, it follows there is no biblical authority for a special group of men who have the power to forgive our sins through confession and absolution and thus reconcile us to God.

To be a priest who absolves a person from the guilt of sin is to be a mediator, one who reconciles two parties together. But, as we have seen, the Bible teaches that there is only *one mediator* between God and man, the man Christ Jesus.

John Hardon S.J. says, 'Penance is the sacrament instituted by Christ in which sinners are reconciled with God through the absolution of the priest' (*The Question and Answer Catholic Catechism*, 1321).

For penance and absolution to be a reality there must be a priest. He alone, according to the Roman Catholic Church, has the authority to hear confession and forgive sins. But since the Bible teaches there is no more priesthood, it follows that there is no biblical authority for either confession to a priest or penance.

Since a human priesthood exists no longer, the particular interpretation the Roman Catholic Church gives to Matthew 16:16–19 (and also to John 20:23) is incorrect. Its whole concept of confession and penance is completely contrary to the teaching of the Bible. And this is true not only of the Roman Catholic teaching on human priesthood, but also on the work of Jesus Christ.

To appreciate why this is so we need to understand what the Bible teaches concerning Christ's sacrifice for sin. In the section on the Mass we saw that when the Lord Jesus was sacrificed on the cross, he paid the *complete* penalty for sins, not merely the penalty for the original sin of Adam. Christ endured the wrath of God against specific sins. He became our substitute: 'He Himself bore our *sins* in His body on the cross' (*1 Pet. 2:24*). 'Sins' means every transgression of the Law of God that we have committed in thought, word, deed, and motive.

In this sense Jesus Christ is 'the *propitiation* for our sins; and not for ours only, but also for those of the whole world' (*1 Jn. 2:2*). Propitiation means the satisfying of wrath. Jesus Christ has borne the wrath and judgment of God for all our sins on the cross. Because he has paid the complete penalty for them no more sacrifices are necessary. *All* our transgressions were placed on Christ and their *entire* penalty was paid by him. This is clearly taught in Colossians 2:13–14: 'And when you were dead in your transgressions and the uncircumcision of your flesh, He made you alive together with Him, having *forgiven* us *all* our transgressions, having cancelled out the certificate of debt consisting of decrees against us and which was hostile to us; and He has taken it out of the way, having nailed it to the cross.'

Paul says 'having forgiven us *all* our transgressions'. Complete forgiveness of sins is found in the work of Jesus Christ on the cross. His blood alone can deal with the guilt of our sins. This is why he alone can be the Saviour. There can be no adding of human works or merit to his work. But the Roman Catholic Church teaches that individuals can atone for their own sins through participation in the sacraments and other forms of human merit. John Hardon S.J. says:

> We make satisfaction for our sins by every good act we perform in the state of grace, but especially by prayer, penance, and the practice of charity. While all prayer merits satisfaction for sin, it is most effective when we ask God to have mercy on us, and unite our prayers with voluntary self-denial. Penance for sin is not only bodily, like fast and abstinence, but also spiritual, like restraining curiosity or conversation and avoiding otherwise legitimate recreation. Moreover, the patient acceptance of trials or humiliations sent by God is expiatory. Finally, the practice of charity toward others is a powerful satisfaction for our lack of charity toward God . . .
>
> Sin can also be expiated through indulgences (*The Question and Answer Catholic Catechism*, 1392, 1400).

But this concept is totally foreign to the Bible.

The Roman Catholic Church also teaches that there is a distinction for the Christian between different kinds of sins, which it terms mortal and venial. Mortal sin is sin worthy of hell, while venial sin is not as serious and will merely relegate a person to a specific time in purgatory. Thus the Roman Church teaches that there are two kinds of punishment due to sin, one eternal and the other temporal. But the terms 'mortal' and 'venial' are never used in Scripture. Neither does the Bible distinguish between eternal punishment and temporal punishment. These are completely arbitrary distinctions by the Roman Catholic Church which have no authority in the Word of God.

Some may argue at this point that 1 John 5:16–17, while not using the specific terms 'mortal' and 'venial', certainly seems to use similar concepts. John says:

> If anyone sees his brother committing a sin not leading to death, he shall ask and God will for him give life to those who commit sin not leading to death. There is a sin leading to death; I do not say that he should make request for this. All unrighteousness is sin, and there is a sin not leading to death.

But do these verses support the teaching of the Roman Catholic Church that for the Christian there is the possibility of committing sin which is mortal, that is, which results in the loss of eternal life and results in eternal death? Not if these verses are properly interpreted within the context of 1 John and the broader context of the rest of Scripture.

Within this Epistle, John uses the term 'brother' in the broad sense of someone who makes a profession of being a Christian. The presence of true faith is thus assumed, but not guaranteed. For example, in 1 John 2:11 John says that 'the one who hates his brother is in the darkness and walks in the darkness'. He tells us further, 'Everyone who hates his brother is a murderer; and you know that no murderer has eternal life abiding in him' (*1 Jn. 3:15*). Even though such an individual claims to be a Christian and a brother, if his life is characterised by hatred, he cannot be a true Christian. He does not have eternal life abiding in him. By contrast, a genuine Christian is one who possesses eternal life that can never be lost: 'My sheep hear My voice, and I know them, and they follow Me; and I give eternal life to them, and they shall never perish; and no one shall snatch them out of My hand. My Father, who has given them to Me, is greater than all; and no one is able to snatch them out of the Father's hand' (*Jn. 10:27–29*). Those who become Christians can never perish. Eternal life is *eternal*; it is permanent.

In addition to this a true Christian will not practise or live in sin: 'No one who is born of God practises sin, because His seed abides in him; and he cannot sin, because he is born of God' (*1 Jn. 3:9*). This is not to say that a Christian is perfect and will never sin. What it means is that the bent of a true Christian's life is not towards sin, but towards holiness. In 1 Corinthians 6, Galatians 5, and Ephesians 5, Paul underlines that those whose lives are marked by the sins he lists in these chapters will not inherit the kingdom of God. He is not saying that these people were Christians who committed mortal sin and subsequently lost their salvation. Rather they were never Christians to begin with, for they practise sin while 'no one born of God practises sin'. They have never been born of God, even though they may profess to be Christians.

Thus a Christian cannot commit a sin unto death in the sense of eternal death. In these verses John is talking about those who, though they may have professed Christ, have never genuinely experienced new birth. In fact, one reason for his letter is to warn true believers against those who were deceivers and false teachers. They claimed to be Christians but their lives were inconsistent with their profession. They walked in darkness (*1:6*); they did not keep the commandments of God (*2:3–4*); they loved the world (*2:15–17*); they lived in unrighteousness and sin (*3:4–10*); they did not love (*3:14–19*); and they denied basic truths about the person of Jesus Christ (*2:22–23; 4:2–3; 5:1*). These men knew the truth, but they had either completely rejected it and gone into apostasy or embraced a life-style of open and deliberate sin. It is probably to these that John is referring when he speaks of certain individuals committing 'sin unto death'. This interpretation is consistent with the teaching of other passages of Scripture. For example, Hebrews 6:4–6 and 10:26 speak of individuals who, after having come to a knowledge of the truth, have turned away from the faith into total apostasy. It is impossible for them to be renewed again to repentance. All they can look forward to in the future is the judgment of God. Again, Matthew 12:22–32 records an incident when the Pharisees attributed the works of Jesus to the devil. This is a deliberate refusal of truth and an ascribing the work of the Holy Spirit to Satan. Jesus says they are guilty of an eternal sin, which can never be forgiven, for they have completely hardened their hearts against the witness of the Holy Spirit to Christ. They will die in their sins eternally separated from God (*Jn. 8:24*). They have committed a sin unto death.

When John uses the term 'sin not unto death' what he means is that the doom of such people is not sealed. There is still time for them to repent and find forgiveness. When Paul says that certain people whose lives are characterised by sin will not inherit the kingdom of God, he is not saying that such people cannot repent and find forgiveness. What he means is that if they die in that unrepentant state, never having been cleansed by the blood of Jesus, then their doom is sealed when they die. Up to the point of death they have opportunity for repentance. The person, however, who commits a sin unto death has at that point sealed his doom. For that person there is no more opportunity for repentance. This is what happened to a number of the Pharisees of Jesus' day.

Thus John is not dealing with genuine Christians in this passage at all, but with those who are counterfeits, or are false teachers. It is impossible for a Christian to commit a mortal sin in the way in which the Roman Catholic Church suggests, for true believers can never lose eternal life, and will not live in sin or apostatise from the faith.

The truth is that, ultimately, there is no distinction such as mortal and venial sin made in the Bible. All sin in God's eyes is mortal and condemns to hell. The consequences in the human realm for certain kinds of sin will differ but the ultimate consequences are the same for all sin – eternal death:

'The wages of sin is death' (*Rom. 6:23*); 'The person who sins will die' (*Ezek. 18:20*).

If the penalty for all sin is eternal death, then there is no distinction to be made between eternal and merely temporal punishment due to sin. Consequently there is no such place as purgatory where a person must go after death to suffer temporal punishment for sins. There is no merely temporal punishment due to sin. It is all eternal. Since Christ has paid that penalty in full for his people, to teach that there is a purgatory where they must be punished for venial sin is to deny the sufficiency of the work of Christ and to believe that the individual can and must add his sufferings to the sufferings of Christ in order to be saved.

Scripture nowhere teaches the doctrine of purgatory. That again is an arbitrary teaching of the Roman Catholic Church. In contrast, the Bible teaches that when an individual comes to Jesus Christ in repentance and faith, he is immediately set free from all judgment, punishment, and condemnation for sin. He is immediately given the gift of eternal life and may have the absolute assurance that he will go to heaven when he dies: 'There is therefore now *no condemnation* for those who are in Christ Jesus' (*Rom. 8:1*); 'Truly, truly, I say to you, he who hears My word, and believes Him who sent Me, *has eternal life*, and does not come into judgment, but has passed out of death into life' (*Jn. 5:24*). When a person believes in Jesus Christ his sins are completely dealt with and the punishment due for them paid in full.

No priest can absolve us from the guilt of our sins and give us acceptance with God. No amount of good works can atone for the punishment due for our sins. Only the blood of God's Son can adequately atone for our sin. The following Scriptures provide clear proof of this:

> Without shedding of *blood* there is no forgiveness (*Heb. 9:22*).

The *blood* of Jesus His Son cleanses us from all sin (*1 Jn. 1:7*).

In Him we have redemption through His *blood*, the forgiveness of our trespasses, according to the riches of His grace (*Eph. 1:7*).

Knowing that you were not redeemed with perishable things like silver or gold from your futile way of life inherited from your forefathers, but with precious *blood*, as of a lamb unblemished and spotless, the blood of Christ (*1 Pet. 1:18–19*).

Much more then, having now been justified by His *blood*, we shall be saved from the wrath of God through Him (*Rom. 5:9*).

For if the blood of goats and bulls and the ashes of a heifer sprinkling those who have been defiled, sanctify for the cleansing of the flesh, how much more will the *blood* of Christ, who through the eternal Spirit offered Himself without blemish to God, *cleanse* your conscience from dead works to serve the living God? (*Heb. 9:13–14*).

Forgiveness and acceptance with God have absolutely nothing to do with human effort and good works. They are accomplished solely on the basis of Christ's dying on the cross, shedding his blood there, and rising again. Man's responsibility is simply to acknowledge the sufficiency of that work, to acknowledge his own bankruptcy and inability to do anything to merit God's favour, and to turn in faith to receive the Lord Jesus as Lord and Saviour. This is why the Bible tells us that we are justified by faith and not by the works of the Law. All our efforts to keep the Law end only in condemnation: 'Now we know that whatever the Law says, it speaks to those who are under the Law, that every mouth may be closed, and all the world may become accountable to God; because by the works of the Law no flesh will be justified in His sight; for through the Law comes the knowledge of sin' (*Rom. 3:19–20*).

The apostle Paul insists that it is 'by grace you have been saved through *faith*; and that not of yourselves, it is the gift of God; *not* as a result of *works*, that no one should boast' (*Eph. 2:8*). It is by *grace* that a man is saved through *faith*. This completely cancels out all works. For 'grace' means the unmerited favour of God. God accepts a man and brings him into his favour through faith in the finished work of Jesus Christ, and not on the basis of human merit.

Paul carefully demonstrates this in his Letter to the Romans: 'For if Abraham was justified by works, he has something to boast about; but not before God. For what does the Scripture say? "And Abraham *believed* God, and it was reckoned to him as righteousness." But to the one who does *not* work, but *believes* in Him who justifies the ungodly, his *faith* is reckoned as righteousness' (*Rom. 4:2,3,5*); 'For we maintain that a man is justified by *faith* apart from works of the Law' (*Rom. 3:28*); 'Therefore having been *justified by faith*, we have peace with God through our Lord Jesus Christ' (*Rom. 5:1*). The Word of God teaches that salvation comes to a person totally apart from works of any kind. An individual is justified by faith.

At this point an objection might be raised. Doesn't James chapter 2 say that an individual is justified by works and not by faith alone? This apparent contradiction is resolved when we recognize that James and Paul are speaking about salvation from two different perspectives. Yet both are able to appeal to the same Old Testament text (*Jas.2:23; Rom. 4:3*). James is dealing with the kind of faith necessary for salvation (i.e. living faith versus dead faith). Paul, on the other hand, is dealing with how a man receives justification (i.e. how a man is made right with God).

Paul is saying that a person is saved by grace through faith completely apart from the works of the Law. James is saying that true saving faith will always result in a holy life. Once a man has been justified his life will radically change. James is warning his readers against the danger of a so-called faith that is empty and dead, which does not result in a changed life. He says in effect that if a man says he has faith but has no works, that kind of 'faith' will never save him. No man can be saved and continue living in sin. True saving faith will always result in a changed life – a life of good works. But those good works are not the basis upon which a man or woman merits salvation. They are *not the cause*, but the *result* of being saved.

It is also important to make a distinction between acceptance with God and fellowship with God. A Christian's acceptance with God is something which is eternally secured in Jesus Christ. A person can never lose this salvation because it is based upon Christ's work. He has paid the entire penalty for all sin.

But sin can and does affect the Christian's enjoyment of fellowship with God. How then is sin to be dealt with and how is fellowship with God to be restored? By confession of that sin directly to God through Jesus Christ, since he is our priest and the only mediator between ourselves and God. We do not go through human mediators. We go through Jesus *alone* because the human priesthood has been abolished. And where there is confession of sin and true repentance, the Christian experiences immediate forgiveness and restoration to fellowship with God, his Father: 'If we confess our sins, He is faithful and righteous to forgive us our sins and to cleanse us from all unrighteousness' (*1 Jn. 1:9*).

Forgiveness and cleansing are secured exclusively on the basis of the blood of the Lord Jesus Christ. God will never forgive us and restore us to fellowship with himself because of good works or penance. God can never accept our good works as a payment for sin. To do so would be to dishonour the perfect work of his Son. God's way is for an individual to confess his sin directly to him, repent of it, and then receive by faith the cleansing of the blood of Jesus Christ. Penance can never be a payment for sin.

But according to the Roman Catholic Church the Bible commands that we do penance. The Bible translation used by the Council of Trent, the Latin Vulgate, expresses this teaching:

> *Ezekiel 18:30*: Be converted and *do penance* for all your iniquities, and iniquity shall not be your ruin.
>
> *Luke 13:5*: Except you *do penance* you shall all likewise perish.
>
> *Acts 2:38*: *Do penance* and be baptized every one of you.

An examination of the original Hebrew and Greek text of the Old and New Testaments makes it apparent that the Latin Vulgate rendering is an improper translation of these verses. In each case the word translated 'do penance' means repent. In Ezekiel 18:30, it is the Hebrew word *shub* which means to turn, to return, or to repent. It is the same word used in Isaiah 45:22: '*Turn* to Me, and be saved, all the ends of the earth.'

In Luke 13:5 and Acts 2:38 the Greek word the Roman Catholic Church translates as 'do penance' is *metanoeo*, literally meaning 'To change one's mind, i.e. to repent . . . to change one's mind for the better, heartily to amend with abhorrence of one's past sins' (Thayer's *Greek–English Lexicon of the New Testament*). Repentance means recognising sin as an offence to God and resolutely determining in the heart to forsake sin completely and to live in holiness before God. But that is a completely different concept from trying to expiate the guilt and punishment for sin through penance and good works. God wants *repentance*, not penance. To try to do penance to appease God, is to attempt to replace the work of Christ with your own works. It is also to say that his work is insufficient.

To be fair in accurately presenting what the Roman Catholic Church teaches, it is important to point out that more modern translations of the Scriptures by the Roman Church accurately use the word 'repentance'. But such is the influence of the Church's tradition that the meaning communicated by that word carries the same idea as the word 'penance'. The two are synonymous terms in Roman Catholic theology. This is very clearly demonstrated by the statements made by John Hardon S.J. in his *Question and Answer Catholic Catechism*: 'Penance means repentance or satisfaction for sin . . . The virtue of *penance* is necessary for a sinner to be reconciled with God. If we expect his forgiveness, we must *repent*. Penance is also necessary because we must expiate and make reparation for the punishment which is due for our sins. That is why Christ tells us, "Unless you repent you will all perish" (Luke 13:5)' (1318, 1320).

Even though the incorrect translation used by the Council of Trent may have been abandoned, the concept of penance is still retained. It is not enough to use biblical words, but the meaning that we give to those words must be in accordance with the meaning the Bible gives them. The Roman Catholic Church uses the word 'repentance' to mean something quite different from the biblical meaning, and in so doing it leads men and women to trust in their own works rather than in the finished work of Christ. The word of God has been replaced by the word of man, because the work of God has been displaced by the work of man.

THE TRUE MEANING OF MATTHEW 16:18–19

If, in Matthew 16:18–19 and John 20:23, the Lord Jesus Christ was not giving Peter and the other disciples authority to forgive sins through confession and penance, what exactly was he authorising them to do? What does he mean when he uses the terms 'keys of the kingdom' and 'binding' and 'loosing'?

In Matthew 23:2,3,13 we read Jesus' words about the scribes and Pharisees:

> The scribes and the Pharisees have seated themselves in the chair of Moses; therefore all that they tell you, do and observe, but do not do according to their deeds; for they say things, and do not do them . . . But woe to you, scribes and Pharisees, hypocrites, because you shut off the kingdom of heaven from men; for you do not enter in yourselves, nor do you allow those who are entering to go in.

Loraine Boettner's comments on these verses are very helpful at this point.

> The scribes and Pharisees were in possession of the law. In that sense they sat on Moses' seat. As the law was faithfully given to the people, or withheld from them, the way to heaven was opened before them, or closed to them. In the failure of the scribes and Pharisees to give the law to the people they were shutting the kingdom of heaven against men, not literally, but figuratively.
>
> 'The keys of the kingdom' was a symbolic expression for the Old Testament Scriptures which set forth the way of salvation. The Old Testament, of course, was the only Scripture they had at that time. It was the responsibility of the scribes and Pharisees, who were the custodians of the Scriptures to acquaint the people with that knowledge by making the Scripture truth available to them. Instead, they not only neglected that duty but actually veiled the Scriptures and perverted their meaning so that the people who wanted that knowledge were deprived of it. Similarly, in the Christian dispensation, the apostles were given the 'keys of the kingdom,' (clearly not a set of metallic keys), not that they could by a mere word admit certain individuals into the kingdom while excluding others, but that, in the words of Paul, they were 'entrusted with the Gospel' (I Thess. 2:4), and so opened or closed the kingdom as they proclaimed the Word of Life or withheld

> it. In that sense every minister today, and indeed every Christian, who teaches the Word also possesses the 'keys' and admits to, or excludes from, the kingdom. The key to the kingdom is *the Gospel of Christ*. Peter was given that key, and he used it to unlock the kingdom to those to whom he preached. We have that same key, and we must use it in the same way, by making known the message of salvation and so opening up to others the way into the kingdom of heaven.
>
> The powers of binding or loosing, and of forgiving or retaining sins, were given to the apostles as proclaimers of the Word of God, not as priests. As we have shown elsewhere, there is no select class of Christian 'priests' in the New Testament dispensation. The apostles never claimed the power of forgiving sins by absolution as the Roman priests do. Rather they preached the Gospel of salvation through Christ – which was a declarative power, by which they announced the gracious terms on which salvation was granted to sinful men (*Roman Catholicism*, pp. 208–9).

In Matthew 16:18–19 the authority given to Peter, and later to the disciples in general, has to do with the gates of hell not prevailing against the ongoing of the kingdom of God. This is the context in which the words of Jesus were spoken. Jesus said, 'I will build My church; and the gates of Hades shall not overpower it' (*Matt. 16:18*).

The building of the church and the furthering of the kingdom has to do specifically with men and women coming into the kingdom of God. How do men and women enter into the kingdom of God? When men hear the message of the gospel and respond by turning to Jesus Christ in repentance and faith, then they are immediately brought into the kingdom of God. They receive eternal life and the complete forgiveness of sins. Matthew 16:18–19 has absolutely nothing to do with confession and penance but with the authority to declare the gospel of Christ to sinners and to offer them the free forgiveness of sins through repentance and faith in the Lord Jesus Christ.

We can see that this is precisely how the apostles understood the commission of Jesus by noting what Jesus told them to do, and what the apostles actually did in the light of their commission by the Lord Jesus.

Jesus authorised the disciples to preach repentance for the remission of sins in his name to all the nations: 'Thus it is written, that the Christ should suffer and rise again from the dead the third day; and that repentance for forgiveness of sins should be proclaimed in His name to all the nations, beginning from Jerusalem' (*Lk. 24:46–47*).

We are told that the purpose for which the Lord Jesus came into the world was 'to seek and to save that which was lost' (*Lk. 19:10*) and 'to call sinners to repentance' (*Lk. 5:32*). This was his commission from his Father. When he in turn commissioned his disciples, he told them, 'As the Father has sent Me, I also send you' (*Jn.20:21*). In John 17:18 the Lord Jesus says, 'As Thou didst send Me into the world, I also have sent them into the world.' Thus, the disciples were commissioned to go forth, even as Christ himself went forth to seek and save the lost by proclaiming the gospel to men and calling them to repentance and faith.

We are told in Mark 1:14–15 that 'Jesus came into Galilee, preaching the gospel of God, and saying, "The time is fulfilled, and the kingdom of God is at hand; *repent* and *believe* in the gospel".' The gospel is an authoritative message that is to be preached to men. It is the proclamation of the person and work of Jesus Christ and the call to men to repent and believe with respect to his person and work on their behalf.

This is what the Lord Jesus Christ commissioned his disciples to do. And as we look closely at the recorded history of the activity of the apostles in the Book of Acts this is precisely what we find. We find them proclaiming the gospel and calling men to repentance and faith; not hearing confession and commanding men to do penance. Nowhere in the Bible is it ever recorded that the apostles forgave sins by means of such auricular confession.

The following are samples from the Book of Acts of what the disciples preached. They show clearly what they understood the commission of Jesus to be:

> 'Therefore let all of the house of Israel know for certain that God has made Him both Lord and Christ – this Jesus whom you crucified.' Now when they heard this, they were pierced to the heart, and said to Peter and the rest of the apostles, 'Brethren, what shall we do?' And Peter said to them, 'Repent, and let each of you be baptized in the name of Jesus Christ for the forgiveness of your sins' (*2:36–38*).

> But you disowned the Holy and Righteous One, and asked for a murderer to be granted to you, but put to death the Prince of life, the one whom God raised from the dead, a fact to which we are witnesses. Repent therefore and return, that your sins may be wiped away, in order that times of refreshing may come from the presence of the Lord (*3:14,15,19*).

> And there is salvation in no one else; for there is no other name under heaven that has been given among men, by which we must be saved (*4:12*).

> And He ordered us to preach to the people, and solemnly to testify that this is the One who has been appointed by God as Judge of the living and the dead. Of Him all the prophets bear witness that through His name everyone who believes in Him receives forgiveness of sins (*10:42–43*).

> Therefore let it be known to you, brethren, that through Him forgiveness of sins is proclaimed to you, and through Him everyone who believes is freed from all things, from which you could not be freed through the Law of Moses (*13:38–39*).

> They . . . fled to the cities of Lycaonia, Lystra and Derbe, and the surrounding region; and there they continued to preach the gospel (*14:6–7*).

> Therefore having overlooked the times of ignorance, God is now declaring to men that all everywhere should repent, because He has fixed a day in which He will judge the world in righteousness through a Man whom He has appointed, having furnished proof to all men by raising Him from the dead (*17:30–31*).

> I did not shrink from declaring to you anything that was profitable, and teaching you publicly and from house to house, solemnly testifying to both Jews and Greeks of repentance toward God and faith in our Lord Jesus Christ (*20:20–21*).

From these Scriptures it is clear that the apostles understood the commission from Jesus to mean the authority to proclaim the forgiveness of sins to sinners by the heralding of the gospel message. It had nothing to do with the authority of priests to hear confession and through absolution to forgive sins and assign penances.

The Roman Catholic Church teaches the need for priests, confession, and penance as a result of misinterpreting the Word of God. It teaches that Christ established the apostles as priests with authority to sacrifice and forgive sins, while the Word of God teaches that all such priesthood has been completely abolished along with all sacrifices since the sacrifice of Christ is a once-for-all sacrifice dealing completely with the penalty for sin. But the Roman Catholic Church teaches that the sacrifice of Jesus Christ is not an adequate sacrifice in that it has not completely remitted *all* the punishment due to sin.

Consequently Roman Catholic teaching requires faith plus works for justification. It teaches that the merits won for us on the cross by Christ must be channelled and applied to us through the sacraments which priests alone can administer. Then, in addition, they must be merited by ourselves through our own works, moral life, prayers, fastings, sufferings, and penances. All of this replaces the work of Jesus Christ by the work of man. The net result is that men and women put their faith in a church and their own moral and religious works rather than in the person of Jesus Christ himself. This is why the Church calls itself the 'Universal Sacrament of Salvation'. But its teaching on the priesthood, sin, confession, penance, indulgences, purgatory, and forgiveness is a direct contradiction of the teaching of the Bible. Rome teaches faith in Jesus Christ *plus* faith in a church and human merit or works if we are to receive forgiveness and acceptance with God. By contrast the Bible teaches faith in the person and finished work of Jesus Christ *alone*.

Clearly the Roman Catholic Church has fallen into the same error as that of the scribes and Pharisees during the days of Jesus. It has become guilty of teaching as doctrines the precepts of men (*Mk. 7:7*). Jesus told certain people in his day that they were guilty of 'invalidating the word of God by . . . tradition' (*Mk. 7:13*). Since these teachings on the Mass, the Priesthood, Confession, and Penance are contradictory to the Word of God, they cannot be biblical doctrines but are the teachings and traditions which men have devised. They have been elevated to a position of authority equal to the Word of God itself. But the actual effect of these teachings is to invalidate what the Word of God teaches about the sacrifice of Jesus Christ, about the priesthood, about forgiveness of sins and the way of salvation.

Men do not need the sacrifice of a Mass. Jesus is the complete sacrifice. They do not need the mediation of a priest; Jesus is their priest, the only mediator between man and God. They do not need penance to receive cleansing and forgiveness for sins; Jesus' blood alone can wash them and make them clean.

What, then, do I need to do, if penance will not help me? Turn from your sins in repentance and trust in Christ as your only sacrifice and priest. Receive him into your life as your Saviour and submit to him as your Lord. Jesus said: 'Come to *Me*, all who are weary and heavy laden, and I will give you rest. Take My yoke upon you, and learn from Me, for I am gentle and humble in heart; and you shall find rest for your souls' (*Matt. 11:28–29*).

5: *The Eucharist*

AUTHORITATIVE STATEMENTS OF ROMAN CATHOLIC TEACHING ON THE EUCHARIST[1]

The Council of Trent

Session XIII: On the Most Holy Sacrament of the Eucharist

Canon I. If any one denieth, that, in the sacrament of the most holy Eucharist, are contained truly, really, and substantially, the body and blood together with the soul and divinity of our Lord Jesus Christ, and consequently the whole Christ; but saith that he is only therein as in a sign, or in figure, or virtue: let him be anathema.

Canon II. If any one saith, that, in the sacred and holy sacrament of the Eucharist, the substance of the bread and wine remains conjointly with the body and blood of our Lord Jesus Christ, and denieth that wonderful and singular conversion of the whole substance of the bread into the body, and of the whole substance of the wine into the blood – the species only of the bread and wine remaining – which conversion indeed the Catholic Church most aptly calls Transubstantiation: let him be anathema.

The Question and Answer Catholic Catechism

1212. What is the center of the whole Catholic liturgy?

The center of the whole Catholic liturgy is the Eucharist. The Eucharist is most important in the life of the Church because it is

[1] A list of authoritative statements of Roman Catholic teaching on the Eucharist will be found in Appendix E, pp. 157ff.

Jesus Christ. It is the Incarnation continued in space and time. The other sacraments and all the Church's ministries and apostolates are directed toward the Eucharist.

1214. What is the sacrament of the Eucharist?

The Eucharist is a sacrament which really, truly, and substantially contains the body and blood, soul, and divinity of our Lord Jesus Christ under the appearances of bread and wine. It is the great sacrament of God's love in which Christ is eaten, the mind is filled with grace, and a pledge is given to us of future glory.

1217. Is the Eucharist necessary for salvation?

The Eucharist is necessary for salvation, to be received either sacramentally or in desire. Christ's words, 'if you do not eat the flesh of the Son of Man and drink his blood, you will not have life in you' (John 6:53), *mean that Holy Communion is necessary to sustain the life of grace in a person who has reached the age of reason.*

1223. Is only the substance of Christ's human nature present in the Eucharist?

Christ is present in the Eucharist not only with everything that makes him man, but with all that makes him this human being. He is therefore present with all his physical properties, hands and feet and head and human heart. He is present with his human soul, with his thoughts, desires, and human affections.

1224. How does Christ become present in the Eucharist?

Christ becomes present in the Eucharist by means of transubstantiation. Transubstantiation is the term used to identify the change that takes place at the consecration.

SUMMARY OF ROMAN CATHOLIC TEACHING

From the quotations given from the authoritative Roman Catholic sources, we learn that the Eucharist is the sacrament in which the priest has the power to transform the bread and wine into the literal body and blood of Jesus Christ, a process known as transubstantiation. According to Roman Catholic teaching this enables the priest to offer Christ himself to the people to consume and eat literally, as well as to offer him on the altar in sacrifice. The Church derives this teaching from its interpretation of the passages in the Gospels dealing with the Last Supper and also from John chapter 6 where Jesus speaks of eating his flesh and drinking his blood.

When the Roman Catholic Church uses the term 'Eucharist' it quite often attaches to it the word 'sacrifice' to form the phrase 'Eucharistic Sacrifice.' Thus, essential to the Eucharist is the idea of sacrifice. According to the Second Vatican Council this is the major purpose of Christ in instituting the Eucharist: 'At the Last Supper, on the night when He was betrayed, our Savior instituted the Eucharistic Sacrifice of His Body and Blood. He did this in order to perpetuate the sacrifice of the Cross throughout the centuries until He should come again . . .' (*The Documents of Vatican II*, p. 154).

We have already seen that the Bible teaches that there are no longer any sacrifices (*Heb. 10:18*) and the priesthood has been abolished. Consequently the Roman Catholic Church's interpretation of John chapter 6 and those passages related to the Last Supper must be unbiblical. Since there is no priesthood, there cannot be a special power given to a select group of men to enable them to change bread and wine into the literal body and blood of Jesus Christ.

But what exactly do these passages of Scripture mean? John 6:26–65 is the account of an incident where Jesus presents himself to the Jews as the Bread of Life:

> Jesus said to them, 'I am the bread of life; he who comes to Me shall not hunger, and he who *believes* in Me shall never thirst . . . For this is the will of My Father, that everyone who beholds the Son and *believes* in Him, may have eternal life; and I Myself will raise him up on the last day . . . Truly, truly, I say to you, he who *believes* has eternal life. I am the bread of life' (*Jn. 6:35,40,47–48*).

Jesus gives an illustration in order that these people might understand what he means by the word 'believe' which he has used five times in this section: 'This is the bread which comes down out of heaven, so that one may eat of it and not die. I am the living bread that came down out of heaven; *if anyone eats of this bread, he shall live forever*; and the bread also which I shall give for the life of the world is My flesh' (*Jn. 6:50–51*). Then Jesus makes this statement: 'It is the Spirit who gives life; the flesh profits nothing; the words that I have spoken to you are spirit and are life' (*Jn. 6:63*).

Jesus makes it clear that the significance of his words to the Jews is spiritual: 'The words I have spoken to you are spirit. The flesh profits nothing'. They must be interpreted in a spiritual and not in a literal or physical manner. Jesus is teaching them what it means to enter into a spiritual relationship with himself. Thus, when he speaks of them eating his flesh and drinking his blood he is not speaking literally. This is a figurative way of explaining the meaning of faith. True faith is an appropriation of the very life of Jesus Christ himself into our lives so that he personally becomes the very life of our life. Jesus is not literal bread but he calls himself the bread of life. That is figurative language with a spiritual meaning. He goes on to say that 'He who comes to Me shall not hunger, and he who believes in Me shall never thirst.' Here he speaks of coming and believing. What does it mean to come and believe in him? It means coming into a spiritual union with the Son of God, so that it is likened to eating his flesh and drinking his blood. Belief means far more than intellectual assent. It means the appropriation of the very life of the Son of God into my life, demonstrating that true Christian faith involves coming into a vital, living, intimate relationship with a person and not merely assenting to a set of doctrines proposed by a church.

When Jesus spoke to Nicodemus about the necessity of being born again, this Jewish religious teacher misunderstood the spiritual truth as something physical. 'How can I return to my mother's womb and be born again?' In a similar manner, the Roman Catholic Church misinterprets Jesus' words in John 6:53–54. It interprets them in a way that is completely independent of their context and assigns a physical and literal meaning to what was intended to be spiritual and figurative. Jesus himself said, 'The words I have spoken to you are spiritual. The flesh profits nothing.' By taking the verses out of context, the Roman Catholic Church falls into the same error as Nicodemus did, giving a physical interpretation to a spiritual truth.

The entire passage runs from John 6:22 to 6:65, so that any interpretation of Jesus' words in verses 53–54 must include the whole context in which those words are found. To interpret his words without careful reference to their context is bound to give a meaning to his words that he never intended.

John 6:40,47, and 54 are clearly intended to be equivalent statements:

> For this is the will of My Father, that everyone who beholds the Son and *believes* in Him, may have eternal life; and I Myself will raise him up on the last day (*Jn. 6:40*).

> Truly, truly, I say to you, he who *believes* has eternal life (*Jn. 6:47*).

> He who *eats My flesh* and *drinks My blood* has eternal life, and I will raise him up on the last day (*Jn. 6:54*).

The terms 'to eat' and 'to drink' illustrate what it means to believe – and to believe in Christ results in eternal life and in being raised up on the last day. We receive eternal life by exercising faith in Christ where we receive him not physically, but spiritually into our hearts and he becomes our very life: 'But as many as *received* Him, to them He gave the right to become children of God, even to those who believe in His name' (*Jn. 1:12*).

These words could not possibly refer to partaking of the Eucharist because they were spoken at least a year before the Last Supper took place. Jesus was stating the necessity of believing upon him – in the figurative sense of eating his flesh and drinking his blood – in order to receive eternal life, *at the time the words were spoken*, not for some time in the future. He speaks in the present tense: 'unless you eat [i.e. now, in the present], you have no life in you.' Only by taking John 6:53–54 out of context and assigning to it a physical interpretation, and then aligning it with their interpretation of the passages related to the Last Supper, can the Roman Catholic Church arrive at its teaching on Transubstantiation.

Transubstantiation means a change of substance. The Roman Church teaches that the whole substance of bread and wine is changed into the physical body and blood of Jesus Christ. This teaching is based on the words of Jesus in Matthew 26:26–28: 'This is my body, this is My blood.' The Roman Catholic Church teaches that these words are to be taken completely literalistically. They believe that in his command 'Do this in remembrance of Me', Jesus was authorising and empowering the apostles as priests to carry on this practice of transubstantiation, that they might offer Christ to the people to be literally eaten and also to be continually sacrificed for their sins.

However, it becomes obvious that Jesus was not speaking in a literalistic, but in a figurative sense. He did this quite often when teaching and the Bible itself is full of figurative teaching. Loraine Boettner expresses this well:

> We believe that the real meaning of Christ's words can be seen when they are compared with similar figurative language . . .
>
> He said, 'I am the door' (John 10:7) – but obviously He did not mean that He was a literal wooden door with lock and hinges. He said, 'I am the Vine' (John 15:5) – but no one understood Him to mean that He was a grapevine.

> When He said 'I am the good shepherd' (John 10:14), He did not mean that He was actually a shepherd. When He said, 'Ye must be born again' (John 3:7), He referred not to a physical birth but to a spiritual birth. When He said, 'Destroy this temple, and in three days I will raise it up' (John 2:19), He meant His body, not the structure of wood and stone . . . He said, 'Ye are the salt of the earth' (Matt. 5:13), and 'Ye are the light of the world' (Matt. 5:14). He spoke of 'the leaven of the Pharisees and Sadducees' (Matt. 16:6) (*Roman Catholicism*, pp. 177–78).

All through the Old Testament God speaks of himself figuratively, as possessing arms, hands, eyes, and ears. In Psalm 91:4 we read he has 'wings and feathers', but we know that God is Spirit and not physical. He does not have flesh, bones, or feathers. This is figurative language. In a similar way, none of these teachings or statements by Jesus should be taken literally; they are figurative in meaning. So it is with the Lord's Supper. Jesus' words are figurative.

> The accounts of the institution of the Lord's Supper, both in the Gospels and in Paul's letter to the Corinthians, make it perfectly clear that He spoke in figurative terms. Jesus said, 'This cup is the new covenant in my blood' (Luke 22:20). And Paul quotes Jesus as saying: 'This is the new covenant in my blood . . . For as oft as ye eat this bread, and drink the cup, ye proclaim the Lord's death till He come' (I Cor. 11:25–26). In these words He used a double figure of speech. The cup is put for the wine, and the wine is called the new covenant. The cup was not literally the new covenant, although it is declared to be so as definitely as the bread is declared to be His body. They did not literally drink the cup, nor did they literally drink the new covenant . . . Nor was the bread literally His body, or the wine His blood. After giving the wine to the disciples Jesus said, 'I shall not drink from henceforth of the fruit of the vine, until the kingdom of God shall come' (Luke 22:18). So the wine, even as He gave it to them, and after He had

> given it to them, remained 'the fruit of the vine'! Paul too says the bread remains bread: 'Wherefore whosoever shall eat the bread and drink the cup of the Lord in an unworthy manner . . . But let each man prove himself, and let him eat of the bread, and drink of the cup (I Cor. 11:27–28). No change had taken place in the elements. This was after the prayer of consecration, when the Church of Rome supposes the change took place, and Jesus and Paul both declare that the elements still are bread and wine (Boettner, p. 176).

Christ's words to his disciples are not always to be taken in a literalistic manner. He was inaugurating a memorial feast by which the disciples would be able to keep his sacrifice in mind as a continuing remembrance. Jesus' own words, 'Do this in *remembrance* of me', demonstrate that this supper was to be a memorial feast much like the old Jewish Passover. It was to be a supper of remembrance by which Christians would continually keep before them the sacrifice of the Lord on their behalf.

The Roman Catholic Church's teaching on the Eucharist as the literal body and blood of Jesus, and the means whereby he is sacrificed continually on the altar and then offered as the source of eternal life, is completely contradictory to the truth of the Word of God. There is no longer any priesthood or sacrifice and the words of Jesus are figurative and spiritual, rather than literal and physical.

6: *Baptism*

AUTHORITATIVE STATEMENTS OF ROMAN CATHOLIC TEACHING ON BAPTISM[1]

The Council of Trent

Session VII: On the Sacraments in General

Canon V. If anyone saith, that baptism is free, that is, not necessary unto salvation: let him be anathema.

The Question and Answer Catholic Catechism

1140. What is baptism?

Baptism is the sacrament of spiritual rebirth. Through the symbolic action of washing with water and the use of appropriate ritual words, the baptized person is cleansed of all his sins and incorporated into Christ. It was foretold in Ezekiel, 'I shall pour clean water over you and you will be cleansed; I shall cleanse you of all your defilement and all your idols. I shall give you a new heart, and put a new spirit in you' (Ezekiel 36:25–26).

1151. What are the effects of baptism?

The effects of baptism are the removal of the guilt of sin and all punishment due to sin, conferral of the grace of regeneration and the infused virtues, incorporation into Christ and his Church, receiving the baptismal character and the right to heaven.

1152. What sins does baptism take away?

[1] A list of authoritative statements of Roman Catholic teaching on Baptism will be found in Appendix F, pp. 163ff.

Baptism remits the guilt of all sins, that is, it takes away all sins, whether original sin as inherited from Adam at conception, or actual sin as incurred by each person on reaching the age of reason. No matter how frequent, or how grave the actual sins may be, their guilt is all removed at baptism. All of this is the pure gift of God, since St. Paul writes, 'It was for no reason except his own compassion that he saved us, by means of the cleansing water of rebirth' (Titus 3:5).

BAPTISM

In our study of the different teachings of Roman Catholicism, we have come back again and again to a basic principle of biblical interpretation: since the Bible is the infallible Word of God, it cannot contradict itself. God himself is its author and therefore the Bible is internally consistent.

This cannot be emphasised enough, for the neglect of this principle has led the Roman Catholic Church into false teaching and error with respect to the Mass, the Priesthood, Penance, Confession, and the Eucharist. Its entire scheme of salvation is built upon incorrect interpretation of Scripture. This is nowhere more evident than in its teaching on baptism.

From the authoritative sources it is evident that the Roman Catholic Church teaches that when anyone is baptised with water, they are regenerated or born again. By means of water baptism they become Christians. They are born into the family of God and become children of God.

The technical theological term for this teaching is 'baptismal regeneration'. But this teaching is in direct opposition to the teaching of the Word of God.

For example, in 1 John 3:9 we are told the following: 'No one who is born of God practices sin, because His seed abides in him; and he cannot sin, because he is born of God.'

This verse states quite plainly that when an individual is born of God, he or she will not practise sin. This does not mean that those who are born of God will live perfect lives, but they will not *live* in sin. Sin will not be the habitual practice of their lives, for in receiving a new heart they receive a completely new disposition which is oriented towards holiness and hatred for sin. The overall bent of their lives will be characterised by holiness. Nor is this the isolated teaching of just one verse of Scripture, but a major emphasis of the entire New Testament (see for example *Romans 8:4–9, 1 Corinthians 6:9–11, Ephesians 2:1–10; 5:5, Galatians 5:19–21, James 2:14–26, 1 John 2:3–4,15–16; 3:6–10,14; 4:7–8*).

This means that if water baptism causes an individual to be born of God (or regenerated), then every individual who is baptised will live a life of holiness before God. They will not practise sin.

But our own experience and observation of the lives of many who have been baptised by water prove that water baptism does not bring about new birth. There are multitudes of people who have been baptised, and yet live in sin. They practise sin.

I speak from personal experience. I was baptised in the Roman Catholic Church as an infant, and yet as I grew older my life was marked by very obvious sin. I practised sin. I was immoral, rebellious, a liar. I cursed. I swore. I told filthy jokes, read impure literature, lived for myself, and was practically an alcoholic by the time I was nineteen years old. And yet I had been baptised. But obviously, according to the Word of God, baptism did not cause me to be born again, for one who is truly born again does not practise sin. My experience can be multiplied countless times in the experience of others who have been baptised by water, but whose lives have never been changed.

Water baptism does not bring about the new birth. To teach that it does is to contradict the testimony of Scripture as well as the practical experience and testimony of many who have been baptised. But what about those passages of

Scripture that seem to indicate that baptism does indeed produce spiritual life in the heart of a man or woman and causes them to be born again?

When the Bible refers to baptism, it does not always mean water baptism. The Scriptures teach that in addition to water baptism, there is also Spirit baptism, which has nothing to do with water. In this baptism of the Holy Spirit, a person who formerly was separated from Christ is united to him, so that he and Christ become one. Their lives are joined together in an indissoluble union. Paul speaks of this when he says that 'by one Spirit we were all baptized into one body' (*1 Cor. 12:13*). Our lives become united to Christ through the baptising work of the Holy Spirit. But again, this is a spiritual union which is effected by a spiritual baptism, of which water baptism is an outward sign.

This concept of Spirit baptism that is distinct from and independent of water baptism can be seen plainly in the analogy of circumcision. The Word of God tells us that circumcision was instituted by God as a sign and seal of his covenant with Abraham: '. . . and he received the sign of circumcision, a seal of the righteousness of the faith which he had while uncircumcised' (*Rom. 4:11*). D. Martyn Lloyd-Jones gives this explanation of the meaning of circumcision:

> What, then, are the reasons why circumcision was ever given? First, circumcision was an outward sign given to Abraham as a seal of the righteousness which he had received fourteen years before. Now to 'seal' means to authenticate. This is illustrated elsewhere in the Scriptures. You remember that we are told in John 6, verse 27 – 'for him hath God the Father sealed'. All commentators are agreed that that statement refers to our Lord's baptism, and it means that at His baptism He was publicly sealed with the sign of the descent of the Holy Spirit in the form of a dove upon Him. The word 'seal' is used in exactly the same way in referring to the Holy Spirit in

> Ephesians 1:13, 14, 'In whom also after that ye believed (or having believed), ye were sealed with that Holy Spirit of promise, which is the earnest of our inheritance until the redemption of the purchased possession, unto the praise of His glory.' The Holy Spirit seals to us God's promise of our ultimate redemption and of our receiving our great inheritance in glory. Having the Holy Spirit I know that all that God promises to me is already mine in a very real sense. It is sealed to me. What the Apostle is saying here is that in the same way circumcision was given to Abraham as a sign to authenticate the imputation of righteousness to him fourteen years before.
>
> In other words the teaching is, that circumcision of itself did not do anything to Abraham. The real reason for it was that Abraham should have the promise made sure to him; it was to seal it to him. And so we are right in saying that circumcision played no part in Abraham's justification. Indeed it is exactly the other way round. Justification is the basis upon which circumcision is given (*Romans: Atonement and Justification*, 1970, pp. 184–85).

Circumcision was meant to be nothing more than a sign and a seal. An outward sign of the inward reality of faith which was already in Abraham's heart, and a seal to him of the promise of God. Romans 4:9–12 makes it clear that circumcision was not the cause of Abraham's regeneration and justification, for he had been justified by faith before he was circumcised. And the argument of Paul in this fourth chapter of Romans is that forgiveness and acceptance with God come solely by faith completely independent of circumcision. He makes this argument because by the time of Christ the Jews had perverted the meaning of circumcision to the point of teaching that circumcision was the effectual cause of a person's becoming a child of God. But Paul shows the fallacy of this teaching, not only in the example of Abraham, but also by drawing a distinction between outward physical circumcision and an inner spiritual circumcision which is accomplished in the heart by the Spirit:

> For he is not a Jew who is one outwardly; neither is circumcision that which is outward in the flesh. But he is a Jew who is one inwardly; and circumcision is that which is of the heart, by the Spirit, not by the letter; and his praise is not from men, but from God (*Rom. 2:28–29*).

Physical circumcision does not make one a true Jew. A spiritual circumcision in the heart, by the Spirit, is what brings this to pass. As Paul points out here, it is possible to be physically circumcised, yet not spiritually circumcised, and therefore not truly a child of God. True circumcision is a thing of the heart, and the outward physical rite is to signify a spiritual reality in the heart. Charles Hodge makes this point when he says:

> It [circumcision] signifies the cleansing from sin, just as baptism now does. Thus we read even in the Old Testament of the circumcision of the heart. (Deut. x. 16; Jer. iv. 4; Ezek. xliv. 7). Therefore uncircumcised lips are impure lips, and an uncircumcised heart is an unclean heart. (Ex. vi. 12; Lev. xxvi. 41. See, also, Acts vii. 51). Paul says the true circumcision is not that which is outward in the flesh; but that which is inward, of the heart, by the Spirit (Rom. ii. 28, 29) . . . Its main design was to signify and seal the promise of deliverance from sin through the redemption to be effected by the promised seed of Abraham (Charles Hodge, *Systematic Theology*, 1873,Volume III, pp. 554–55).

That which is true for the Jew and circumcision is also true for the Christian and baptism. Simply substitute the word 'Christian' for the word 'Jew' and the word 'baptism' for the word 'circumcision' in Romans 2:28–29:

> For he is not a *Christian* who is one outwardly; neither is *baptism* that which is outward in the flesh. But he is a *Christian* who is one inwardly; and *baptism* is that which is

of the heart, by the Spirit, not by the letter; and his praise is not from men, but from God.

The Jews believed that physical circumcision made one a child of God. Paul denies this and insists that there must be a spiritual circumcision of the heart by the Holy Spirit. The Roman Catholic Church falls into the same error as the Jews by teaching that the physical external rite of water baptism will bring about regeneration and constitute the one baptised a child of God. But it is not physical baptism that brings about the new birth. That can be accomplished only by a baptism with the Spirit by which we are permanently united to the person of Christ. Charles Hodge makes the following comment:

> God is a Spirit, and He requires those who worship Him, to worship Him in spirit and in truth. External rites are declared to be nothing . . . 'He is not a Jew, which is one outwardly; neither is that circumcision, which is outward in the flesh: but he is a Jew, which is one inwardly; and circumcision is that of the heart, in the spirit, and not in the letter; whose praise is not of men, but of God.' (Rom. ii. 28, 29). This is not merely a fact, but a principle. What St. Paul here says of circumcision and of Jews, may be said, and is substantially said by St. Peter in reference to baptism and Christianity. A man who is a Christian outwardly only, is not a Christian; and the baptism which saves, is not the washing of the body with water, but the conversion of the soul (1 Peter iii. 21). The idea that a man's state before God depends on anything external, on birth, on membership in any visible organization, or on any outward rite or ceremony, is utterly abhorrent to the religion of the Bible (*Systematic Theology*, Volume III, p. 521).

Just as circumcision was a sign and seal to Abraham of the spiritual transformation that had taken place in his heart, so baptism in this New Testament dispensation is a sign and seal of a spiritual transformation that takes place in the heart by the Holy Spirit. It is public testimony to the washing from sin and new life which is found in him. But water baptism does not effect this inward change of regeneration; it is simply the public testimony to the fact that such a transformation takes place by the grace of God.

> It is plain that baptism cannot be the ordinary means of regeneration, or the channel of conveying in the first instance the benefits of redemption to the souls of men, because, in the case of adults, faith and repentance are the conditions of baptism. But faith and repentance, according to the Scriptures, are the fruits of regeneration. He who exercises repentance towards God and faith in our Lord Jesus Christ is in a state of salvation before baptism and therefore in a state of regeneration. Regeneration consequently precedes baptism, and cannot be its effect, according to the ordinance of God. That the Apostles did require the profession of faith and repentance before baptism, cannot be denied. This is plain, not only from their recorded practice but also from the nature of the ordinance. Baptism is a profession of faith in the Father, and the Son, and the Holy Spirit; not of a faith to be obtained through the ordinance, but of a faith already entertained. When the Eunuch applied to Philip for baptism, he said: 'If thou believest with all thine heart thou mayest.' Of those who heard Peter's sermon on the day of Pentecost it is said, 'they that gladly received his word were baptized.' (Acts ii. 41) (Charles Hodge, *Systematic Theology*, Volume III, p. 601).

As has already been pointed out, Abraham was a justified man long before he was circumcised. In the same way a true Christian is one who has received an inner Spirit baptism before the actual rite of water baptism is applied. An individual does not submit to water baptism in order to experience regeneration, but does so because regeneration has already taken place. We see this further illustrated for us in the first chapter of the Gospel of John:

> But as many as received Him, to them He gave the right to become children of God, even to those who believe in His name, who were born not of blood, nor of the will of the flesh, nor of the will of man, but of God (*Jn. 1:12–13*).

John refers here to being born of God and becoming children of God. He is speaking about the new birth. He says very clearly that the new birth is directly related to receiving Jesus Christ and believing on him. The new birth is not dependent on water baptism but on a work of the Spirit which results in a person's receiving Jesus Christ into his life. Regeneration can never be dissociated from Jesus Christ himself and coming into a personal relationship with him as Lord and Saviour. The Word of God tells us that the two conditions which must be fulfilled if an individual is to come into a relationship with Jesus Christ are those of repentance and faith, in which an individual turns from sin and embraces Jesus Christ and his all-sufficient sacrifice.

ROMANS 6:3–5

One of the major passages of Scripture which the Roman Catholic Church uses to support its teaching that water baptism results in regeneration is Romans 6:3–5. Those verses read as follows:

> Or do you not know that all of us who have been baptized into Christ Jesus have been baptized into His death? Therefore we have been buried with Him through baptism into death, in order that as Christ was raised from the dead through the glory of the Father, so we too might walk in newness of life. For if we have become united with Him in the likeness of His death, certainly we shall be also in the likeness of His resurrection.

These verses do indeed speak of baptism. But we need to keep in mind that when the Scripture uses the term 'baptism' it always carries the idea of Spirit baptism as its underlying reality. The apostle Peter makes this clear when he says, 'And corresponding to that, baptism now saves you – not the removal of dirt from the flesh, but an appeal to God for a good conscience – through the resurrection of Jesus Christ' (*1 Pet. 3:21*). Peter is careful to guard his readers from the mistaken notion that salvation is derived simply from the application of water to physical flesh, when he specifically says 'not the removal of dirt from the flesh'. And he goes on to connect baptism with the idea of 'an appeal to God for a good conscience, through the resurrection of Jesus Christ'. There is obviously more to be understood in the use of the term 'baptism' than just the administering of water. Matthew Henry brings this out in his comments on this passage:

> Noah's salvation in the ark upon the water prefigured the salvation of all good Christians in the church by baptism; that temporal salvation by the ark was a type, the antitype whereunto is the eternal salvation of believers by baptism, to prevent mistakes about which the apostle declares what he means by saving baptism; not the outward ceremony of washing with water, which, in itself, does no more than put away the filth of the flesh, but it is that baptism wherein there is a faithful answer or restipulation of a resolved good conscience, engaging to believe in, and be entirely devoted to, God, the Father, Son, and Holy Ghost, renouncing at the same time the flesh, the world, and the devil. The baptismal covenant, made and kept, will certainly save us. Washing is the visible sign; this is the thing signified.
>
> The apostle shows that the efficacy of baptism to salvation depends not upon the work done, but upon the resurrection of Christ, which supposes his death, and is the foundation of our faith and hope, to which we are rendered conformable by dying to sin, and rising again to

> holiness and newness of life . . . The external participation of baptism will save no man without an answerable good conscience and conversation. There must be the answer of a good conscience towards God (*Matthew Henry's Commentary on the Whole Bible*, Volume 6, pp. 1026–27).

Here in Romans 6 Paul refers not just to baptism with water, but also to the spiritual reality which underlies the sign of water baptism – the identification with Christ that takes place when an individual is baptised by the Holy Spirit into Christ and the newness of life that results from regeneration. He is not merely describing water baptism here, for the whole point of this chapter is that those who are baptised into Christ, which is what water baptism signifies, are freed from sin and they walk in newness of life as slaves of righteousness (*Rom. 6:4,17–18*). But again, this is not something which is effected through water baptism; it is a supernatural work of the Holy Spirit in the heart of a man or woman.

When Spirit baptism takes place, that individual is joined to Christ and he is identified with Jesus in his death, burial and resurrection. The very life of Christ becomes his life and he is born again. And the result of this union is a completely changed life. The context of Romans 6:3–5 has to do with the impossibility of a Christian living under the domination of sin. The two preceding verses (*Rom. 6:1–2*) read as follows:

> What shall we say then? Are we to continue in sin that grace might increase? May it never be! How shall we who died to sin still live in it?

Paul is saying that because a true Christian has been joined to Jesus Christ through the baptising work of the Holy Spirit, it is impossible for that person to live in sin, or as 1 John 3:9 says, to practise sin.

Romans 6:4 says that the person who has been united to Jesus Christ will walk in 'newness of life' because as Romans 6:5 says he has become 'united in the likeness of His resurrection'. Further, Romans 7:4 tells us that a Christian has been joined to Christ that he might bear fruit for God, which means a righteous or holy life. Thus to be baptised into Christ is to become united with him in his resurrection power and to bear the fruit of holiness or righteousness unto God in one's life. The kind of baptism referred to here in Romans 6 always results in a holy life. This person will not live in sin.

But we have already seen that a person can be baptised with water and still continue to live in sin. Therefore there must be a distinct difference between water baptism and Spirit baptism. Water baptism does not result in the Spirit baptism in which an individual is united to Christ and is born again, for an individual can be baptised with water and still practise sin, whereas the person who is baptised by the Holy Spirit into Christ will *not* practise sin.

This is not to deny the importance of water baptism. But only when it is accompanied by the cleansing power of the Spirit are we saved (see *1 Pet. 3:21*). Water baptism, then, is an outward picture of an inward work of grace by the Holy Spirit. It does not bring about the new birth, but is a public testimony to the necessity and nature of the new birth.

There is, then, a very clear distinction drawn in the Word of God between water baptism and a baptism which is spiritual and effected by the Spirit of God in the heart.

JOHN 3:3–5

This passage of Scripture is one of the passages constantly alluded to by the Roman Catholic Church as a basis for its teaching on baptismal regeneration.

Jesus answered and said to him [Nicodemus], 'Truly,

> truly, I say to you, unless one is born again, he cannot see the kingdom of God.'
>
> Nicodemus said to him, 'How can a man be born when he is old? He cannot enter a second time into his mother's womb and be born, can he?'
>
> Jesus answered, 'Truly, truly, I say to you, unless one is born of water and the Spirit, he cannot enter into the kingdom of God.'

Jesus says we must be born again or we will not enter the kingdom of heaven. He tells Nicodemus that a man must be 'born of water and the Spirit'. What exactly does he mean? Does Jesus mean water baptism by his use of the word 'water'? Three reasons suggest that he does not.

Firstly, Jesus could not mean water baptism here for such an interpretation would cause the Word of God to contradict itself. The Bible teaches that water baptism does not cause a person to be born again. Secondly, Jesus is speaking to Nicodemus, who is a Jew, and Christian baptism had not yet been instituted. Thirdly, because Jesus is speaking to Nicodemus, the term must be interpreted within its context. The term 'water' had a certain significance to Nicodemus, who was not only a Jew, but also steeped in the learning of the Old Testament since he was a leading, if not *the* leading teacher in Israel. In the light of these facts what significance would the term 'water' have for Nicodemus? Professor John Murray's comments on John 3:5 are very helpful at this point:

> Now what religious idea would we expect to be conveyed to the mind of Nicodemus by the use of the word *water*? Of course, the idea associated with the religious use of water in the Old Testament and in that religious tradition and practice which provided the very context of Nicodemus' life and profession! And that simply means the religious import of water in the Old Testament, in the rites of Judaism, and in contemporary practice. When we say this,

there is one answer. The religious use of water, that is to say, the religiously symbolic meaning of water, pointed in one direction, and that direction is purification. All the relevant considerations would conspire to convey to Nicodemus that message. And that message would be focussed in his mind in one central thought, the indispensable necessity of purification for entrance into the kingdom of God.

In the Old Testament water often signified washing and purifying from the pollution of sin (cf. Psalm 51:2,3; Isa. 1:16; Jer. 33:8; Ezek. 36:25; Zech. 13:1) . . .

John 3:5 sets forth the two aspects from which the new birth must be viewed – it purges away the defilement of our hearts and it recreates in newness of life. The two elements of this text – 'born of water' and 'born of the Spirit' – correspond to the two elements of the Old Testament counterpart: 'Then will I sprinkle clean water upon you, and ye shall be clean: from all your filthiness, and from all your idols, will I cleanse you. A new heart also will I give you, and a new spirit will I put within you: and I will take away the stony heart out of your flesh, and I will give you an heart of flesh' (Ezek. 36:25,26). This passage we may properly regard as the Old Testament parallel to John 3:5, and there is neither reason nor warrant for placing any other interpretation upon 'born of water' than that of Ezek. 36:25: 'Then will I sprinkle clean water upon you, and ye shall be clean' (*Collected Writings of John Murray*, Volume 2, 1977, pp. 182–84).

To Nicodemus the term 'water' must have conveyed the idea of cleansing from the guilt and pollution of sin. In John 3:5 the term 'water' refers to cleansing from the guilt of sin, as Paul says, similarly, in Titus 3:5: 'He saved us, not on the basis of deeds which we have done in righteousness, but according to His mercy, by the washing of regeneration and renewing by the Holy Spirit.' This 'washing' takes place through the work of Christ on our behalf (see *Rev. 1:5*).

The basis for our entering the kingdom of God is our

washing, our cleansing, our purification from the guilt and defilement of sin through the blood of Jesus Christ. The agent by which we are actually regenerated is the Spirit of God who communicates new life to us by uniting us to Christ. He thus brings us into the kingdom of God cleansed and made new through the blood of Jesus. This is further amplified in John 3:14–16:

> And as Moses lifted up the serpent in the wilderness, even so must the Son of Man be lifted up; that whoever believes may in Him have eternal life. For God so loved the world, that He gave His only begotten Son, that whoever believes in Him should not perish, but have eternal life.

In Moses' day a bronze serpent was attached to a wooden pole and then lifted up so that those who looked at it would not die. In the same way, God's Son was to be lifted up – that is, nailed to a wooden cross, and lifted up to die for the sins of the world. Thus God so loved the world that he gave his only begotten Son, that those who trust in the sufficiency of that blood sacrifice would not perish eternally, but instead possess eternal life.

To be born again is to possess eternal life. Jesus says that an individual must be born again to enter the kingdom of heaven. The basis upon which a person is born again is Christ's atoning sacrifice on the cross. He was lifted up just as the serpent in the wilderness was. Salvation becomes ours when we exercise faith in this sacrifice. In the context of John 3, therefore, regeneration has nothing to do with water as such.

CONCLUSION

Just as Nicodemus could think only in material terms when Jesus spoke of being 'born again' and he began to speak of entering a second time into his mother's womb, so the

Roman Catholic Church relegates the new birth to a purely mechanical ritual of being sprinkled with physical water and robs it of its spiritual significance and reality.

To do this is completely contradictory to the teaching of the Word of God with respect to baptism and the new birth. Sadly, there are multitudes of people who are deceived into believing that if they have simply been baptised with water then they have been born again. But they make the same error the Jews made during the time of Paul when they equated circumcision with spiritual life. Those Jews, though sincere, were completely wrong in their belief and teaching, and the same can be said today with respect to the Roman Catholic Church's teaching on baptism.

7: *Roman Catholicism, the Judaisers, and the Book of Galatians*

The Roman Catholic Church's teachings on the Mass, the Priesthood, Confession, Penance, the Eucharist, and Baptism all combine to form a system of salvation. The Church claims that if men and women will be baptised in the Catholic Church and adhere to its teachings in these areas, it can lead them in the path of salvation. In Roman Catholic teaching, Baptism, the Mass, the Priesthood, Confession, Penance, and the Eucharist are all necessary for salvation.

However, as we have seen in our studies, there is a huge contrast between the teaching of the Roman Church and the teaching of the Bible. This alone is enough to disqualify the Roman Catholic Church from being a truly Christian church able to direct men in the path of salvation, for the prophet Isaiah says, 'To the law and to the testimony: if they speak not according to this word, it is because there is no light in them' (*Is. 8:20, A.V.*).

Because the teaching of Rome contradicts the teaching of the Word of God on the true way of salvation, we can say conclusively that the Roman Catholic Church teaches a false gospel and a false way of salvation. This can be clearly seen from Paul's teaching in his Letter to the Galatians.

Galatians contains some very strong language. It is a letter of warning and of judgment. Its main theme is the gospel of Christ; its main intent is to defend that gospel from the perversions of false teachers. Certain men who had come into the life of the Galatian church had begun to teach errors about the way of salvation, and to spread a false gospel. Under the inspiration of the Holy Spirit and with intense emotion and indignation, Paul writes a letter in which he defends the true gospel, exposes the error of the false teachers, and utters a divine curse against anyone who distorts the gospel of Jesus Christ.

The gospel which these false teachers espoused is essentially identical with the Roman Catholic Church's teaching on salvation. How can this be demonstrated? Paul begins his letter by defining his concern very clearly:

> I am amazed that you are so quickly deserting Him who called you by the grace of Christ, for a different gospel; which is really not another; only there are some who are disturbing you, and want to distort the gospel of Christ. But even though we, or an angel from heaven, should preach to you a gospel contrary to that which we have preached to you, let him be accursed. As we have said before, so I say again now, if any man is preaching to you a gospel contrary to that which you received, let him be accursed (*Gal. 1:6–9*).

These are very strong words indeed. The false teaching that had been espoused and the teachers themselves had come under a divine curse. Why such severity? Because the issues at stake in the purity of the gospel have to do with the glory of God and the eternal destinies of men and women. If that gospel is in any way distorted or perverted it results in men being eternally damned and it robs God of his glory.

Who were the people whom Paul denounced in the strongest possible terms? And what was the essence of their 'gospel', which made it a distortion of the true gospel? First of all Paul says that the Galatians, in accepting this false teaching, were deserting the God who called them by the *grace* of Christ (*Gal. 1:6*). Grace is unmerited favour. The favour of God towards us cannot be merited by anything we can do: 'The true gospel is in its essence what Paul called it in Acts 20:24, "the gospel of the grace of God" . . . Nothing is due to our efforts, merits or works; everything in salvation is due to the grace of God' (J. R. W. Stott, *The Message of Galatians*, 1968, p. 22).

The false teachers who had invaded this church were a group of Judaisers whose teaching involved an attempt to combine Christianity with the essential elements of the Jewish religion. They taught that a person must believe in Jesus, but in addition they taught that a person also had to be circumcised and keep both the moral and ceremonial laws given through Moses. Paul makes reference in this letter to various elements in the teaching of these Judaisers, including circumcision, the observance of feast days, and the Law of Moses:

> Behold I, Paul, say to you that if you receive circumcision, Christ will be of no benefit to you . . . You have been severed from Christ, you who are seeking to be justified by law; you have fallen from grace . . . For in Christ Jesus neither circumcision nor uncircumcision means anything, but faith working through love (*Gal. 5:2,4,6*).

> Those who desire to make a good showing in the flesh try to compel you to be circumcised, simply that they may not be persecuted for the cross of Christ. For those who are circumcised do not even keep the Law themselves, but they desire to have you circumcised, that they may boast in your flesh. But may it never be that I should boast, except in the cross of our Lord Jesus Christ, through which the world has been crucified to me, and I to the world. For neither is circumcision anything, nor uncircumcision, but a new creation (*Gal. 6:12–15*).

> But now that you have come to know God, or rather to be known by God, how is it that you turn back again to the weak and worthless elemental things, to which you desire to be enslaved all over again? You observe days and

> months and seasons and years. I fear for you, that perhaps I have laboured over you in vain (*Gal. 4:9–11*).

> Nevertheless knowing that a man is not justified by the works of the Law but through faith in Christ Jesus, even we have believed in Christ Jesus, that we may be justified by faith in Christ, and not by the works of the Law; since by the works of the Law shall no flesh be justified . . . I do not nullify the grace of God; for if righteousness comes through the Law, then Christ died needlessly (*Gal. 2:16,21*).

Thus J. R. W. Stott rightly says:

> The false teachers . . . did not deny that you must believe in Jesus for salvation, but they stressed that you must be circumcised and keep the law as well. In other words, you must let Moses finish what Christ has begun . . . You must add your works to the work of Christ. You must finish Christ's unfinished work (p. 22).

But Paul denounces this in no uncertain terms because it is adding human merit to the merit of Christ. It is a system of faith in Christ plus human works. Paul says that this is perverting the gospel of the grace of God.

The Greek word translated 'distort' or 'pervert' can mean 'reverse'. These false teachers were reversing the gospel by radically changing its character. They were presenting a totally different gospel from that which God had given with the result that if a person believed this false gospel he would believe a lie and would perish eternally. Consequently a divine curse, an anathema, was called down upon these false teachers and their teaching. By contrast, the true gospel is the gospel of the grace of God, whereby a man is justified before God and accepted by him solely on the merits of the life, death, and resurrection of Jesus Christ, apart from any human works of merit, and it is received by faith alone.

Throughout Galatians 2:11–16 Paul mentions the truth of

the gospel. What is the truth? 'It is the good news that we sinners, guilty and under the judgment of God, may be pardoned and accepted by His sheer grace, His free and unmerited favour, on the ground of His Son's death and not for any works or merits of our own.' (Stott, p. 54). The Judaisers, however, were totally perverting this teaching of grace by adding the element of human works. It was Jesus plus Judaism. It was not Jesus alone: 'Salvation is a free gift of God, received through faith in Christ crucified, irrespective of any human merit . . . the Judaisers could not accept the principle of . . . "faith alone". They insisted that men must contribute something to their salvation. So they were adding to faith in Jesus "the works of the law" as another essential ground of acceptance with God' (Stott, p. 85).

What do we mean when we say that the Judaisers were adding to faith in Jesus the works of the Law as another essential ground of acceptance with God? Essentially the Judaisers were teaching that for a man to be saved he must not only believe in Jesus as the Son of God and Messiah who had come to die for men's sins, but he must also become a Jew. This meant that a person had to be circumcised and adhere to the entire Mosaic Law with its ceremonies.

For us fully to understand how the Judaisers' teachings perverted the gospel and how they specifically relate to the teachings of Roman Catholicism, it is essential that we understand some of the details of the Temple worship of the Jewish religion. The Temple was an exact replica of the Tabernacle the Jews used for worship in the wilderness except that the Temple was stationary and exactly double the size of the Tabernacle. Exodus chapters 26 to 30 give a detailed description of the Tabernacle, of the articles it contained, and of the worship conducted by the priests and high priest. The Book of Leviticus and Hebrews 9:1–9 also give further details of the Temple worship and all that it involved.

> The Tabernacle was an oblong rectangular structure . . . divided internally into two apartments. One was the Holy of Holies into which no one entered, not even the priest except on very extraordinary occasions . . . In this was placed the mercy seat, surmounted by the cherubim and on it was placed the ark containing the Tables of the Law. In front of these was an outer chamber called the Holy Place . . . appropriated to the use of the priests. In it were placed the golden *candlestick* on one side, the table of *shewbread* opposite and between them in the centre the altar of *incense*.
>
> The court of the Tabernacle was surrounded by canvas screens . . . In the outer half was placed the *altar* of burnt offerings and between it and the tabernacle the *laver* at which the *priests* washed their hands and feet on entering the Temple (*Smith's Dictionary of the Bible*, Volume 4, pp. 3193–95)

The ceremonial worship of the Jews would, therefore, include the following elements: an altar, daily sacrifices, a laver of water, priests, a high priest, special priestly and high priestly vestments and robes (*Ex. 28*), candles, incense, and shewbread. Then, in the routine religious life of the average Jew there would be feast days, the giving of alms, prayers, fastings, and adherence to certain dietary restrictions and laws.

All of these things would be involved in the Judaisers' teaching. It was Jesus *plus* the Jewish system. But how does all this relate to Roman Catholicism? The essence of what the Judaisers taught is included in Roman Catholicism. The same basic error is clothed in a different garment. The Roman Catholic Church teaches that salvation is achieved by believing in Jesus as the Son of God who died for the sins of the world, by being baptised, by joining the Roman Catholic Church, by striving to keep the Ten Commandments, and by partaking of the Sacraments which involves a sacrificial system, altars, priests, a high priest, and the exercise of good works such as prayers, fastings, alms giving, penances, and until recently adherence to certain dietary restrictions.

In his *Question and Answer Catholic Catechism*, John Hardon S.J. makes the following statements about the nature of salvation:

> 412. Is the Church necessary for salvation?
> Yes, the Church is necessary for salvation.
> 492. Is faith in what God revealed sufficient for salvation?
> No, we must also keep his Commandments. As Christ himself told us, 'If you wish to enter into life, keep the commandments.' (Matthew 19:17)
> 493. How do we keep the Commandments of God?
> We keep the Commandments of God by living a good moral life.
> 1119. Are the sacraments necessary for salvation?
> According to the way God has willed that we be saved, the sacraments are necessary for salvation.
> 1074. What is habitual or sanctifying grace?
> Habitual or sanctifying grace is a supernatural quality that dwells in the human soul, by which a person shares in the divine nature, becomes a temple of the Holy Spirit, a friend of God, his adopted child, an heir to the glory of heaven and *able to perform actions meriting eternal life* [emphasis mine].
> 1179. Is baptism of water necessary for salvation?
> It is commonly taught by the church that baptism of water is necessary for salvation for those who have not reached the use of reason.
> 1217. Is the Eucharist necessary for salvation?
> The Eucharist is necessary for salvation, to be received either sacramentally or in desire.[1]

It is quite clear from this that in Roman Catholicism faith in Christ alone is not sufficient for salvation. It is also necessary that one keep the Ten Commandments, be baptised, become a

[1] A list of authoritative statements of Roman Catholic teaching on salvation will be found in Appendix G, pp. 168ff.

member of the Roman Catholic Church, and partake regularly of the sacraments. It is not Jesus alone, but Jesus *plus* all these other things. Significantly, all these other things are practically identical to the Judaisers' system and teachings.

Note the following parallels between Roman Catholicism and the Judaisers:

JUDAISERS	ROMAN CATHOLIC CHURCH
1. Belief in Jesus as the Messiah and Son of God	1. Belief in Jesus as the Messiah and Son of God
2. Circumcision	2. Baptism
3. Become a Jew	3. Become a Roman Catholic
4. Sacrificial System	4. Sacrificial System
5. Priests	5. Priests
6. High Priests	6. Popes
7. Altars	7. Altars
8. Laver of Water	8. Font of Holy Water
9. Feast Days	9. Feast Days
10. Dietary Regulations	10. Dietary Regulations (until recently)
11. Candles	11. Candles
12. Incense	12. Incense
13. Shew Bread	13. Eucharistic Wafer
14. Keep the Ten Commandments	14. Keep the Ten Commandments
15. Traditions of the Elders	15. Traditions of the Church Fathers

The parallel is only too plain. The Roman Catholic teaching on salvation, and therefore its gospel, is essentially what Paul condemns the Judaisers for preaching and upon which he pronounces an anathema. J.R.W. Stott's words bear repeating: 'The Judaisers could not accept the principle of . . . "faith alone". They insisted that men must contribute something to their salvation. So they were adding to faith in Jesus "the works of the law" as another essential ground of acceptance with God' (Stott, p. 85).

Thus, the same charge as the apostle Paul levelled against the Judaisers can also be levelled against the Roman Catholic Church. The message of Galatians applies directly to the Roman Catholic Church because its gospel is the same as that of the Judaisers. This is the reason why there can be no unity between the Roman Catholic Church and those who are true Christians. Paul certainly saw no grounds for unity between himself and the Judaisers. As Stott says, 'When the issue between us is trivial, we must be as pliable as possible. But when the truth of the gospel is at stake, we must stand our ground . . . If men oppose the truth of the gospel, we must not hesitate to oppose them' (Stott, pp. 57–58).

Did Paul consider the Judaisers true Christians? Obviously not! They were perverting the gospel and leading men to perdition. Is the Roman Catholic Church truly Christian? On the basis of all that it teaches contrary to the Bible, and in view of the fact that it is in effect a modern-day Judaising system, the answer would have to be an emphatic *no*!

Just as Paul said that those who accepted the teaching of the Judaisers were deserting the gospel, so do those who adhere to Roman Catholic teaching. Paul said that even if an angel from heaven were to preach the gospel of the Judaisers he should be accursed and rejected. These are severe words, but it is God the Holy Spirit who has inspired them and we must not try to explain them away.

As we face the truth of what Paul is teaching, we are driven to the conclusion: the teachings of Roman Catholicism and those of the Judaisers are in important respects practically identical. On the basis of their own official, authoritative statements of doctrine it is obvious that the teaching of the Roman Catholic Church and of the Word of God stand diametrically opposed to each other. To accept the one you must reject the other. To adhere to the teaching of the Roman Catholic Church on salvation is to accept the teaching of a Judaising system which is denounced by God in Galatians because it is a false gospel. It deceives men into thinking that they are walking in the truth when in fact they have departed from it.

This does not mean that those who teach Roman Catholic doctrine are insincere or purposely deceptive people. The Judaisers were sincere, moral, and extremely religious. But they were terribly deceived. When it comes to the gospel, its truth must be maintained in purity, without any subtractions or additions, and loyalty to that gospel must take precedence over loyalty to people or to a church, for to be disloyal to that gospel is to be disloyal to God. Sincerity is never to be the ultimate test by which we measure the acceptability of a spiritual teacher or an organisation. The ultimate criterion is always consistency with the revealed truth of God's Word. Religious leaders and teachers can be sincere and yet be sincerely wrong.

In the Lord Jesus Christ's dealings with the scribes and Pharisees we find a very sober and heart-searching warning which we do well to consider. It is this: it is possible for an individual to give himself devotedly to a system of religion which calls itself 'Christian', but when tested by Scripture proves not to be true Christianity at all.

If we adhere to the teachings of men which are opposed to the Word of God, then our worship and all our religious life is in vain, no matter how sincere we may be. Our worship must be based on the truth (*Jn. 4:24*).

The Lord Jesus Christ had these words to say about the religious leaders of his day: 'This people honors Me with their lips, but their heart is far away from Me. But *in vain* do they worship Me, teaching as doctrines the precepts of men. Neglecting the commandment of God, you hold to the tradition of men' (*Mk. 7:6–8*). Yet the scribes and Pharisees were not insincere. They were zealous about their religious and moral life. Nevertheless, their worship was in vain. It profited them nothing. It did not bring them to God, for they elevated the teachings of men above the truth of the Bible and they distorted and misinterpreted the Word of God, adhering to the teaching and traditions of men rather than to the truth of the Word of God.

As we have seen, the Roman Catholic Church's teaching on salvation contradicts the Bible. Its teaching is the traditions of men elevated to a position above the Word of God. To adhere to such teaching is to come under the judgment which Jesus spoke against the scribes and Pharisees. It is to worship in vain.

If an individual desires to know God, to experience forgiveness, and to be able to worship him in spirit and in truth, it is essential for him or her to understand what the Bible teaches about salvation, and how it is appropriated. In the next section we shall look closely at true, biblical salvation and what we must do in order to be saved.

PART TWO

The Way of Salvation

8: *Man's Problem Defined*

In the preceding chapters we have seen that the teaching of the Roman Catholic Church on salvation is opposed to the clear teaching of the Word of God. However, it is important not only that we see the specific areas where the Bible contradicts Roman Catholicism, but also that we have a clear understanding of what the true gospel is.

The Bible tells us that the way of salvation is found in the message of the gospel. Paul said, 'For I am not ashamed of the gospel, for *it is the power of God for salvation* to everyone who believes, to the Jew first and also to the Greek' (*Rom. 1:16*). The gospel is God's message of salvation, which centres on the person and work of Jesus Christ. It declares the basis and the means by which men may be delivered from the guilt and power of sin.

If we are going truly to understand the message of the gospel and the work of salvation he has in fact accomplished, we must first of all understand why salvation is necessary.

The Bible teaches us that we have been created by God, and that he sustains us in existence: 'In Him we live and move and exist' (*Acts 17:28*). Furthermore, 'He Himself gives to all life and breath and all things' (*Acts 17:25*). We can breathe, speak, think, and act only because God sustains our lives. All that we are and have is a gift from him alone. The Word of God also makes it clear that men have been created for a specific purpose: 'All things have been created *by* Him and *for* Him' (*Col. 1:16*). We were created to live for his glory and to do his will. But men have rejected the purpose for which they were created. They live for themselves rather than for the glory of God. This is what the Bible defines as the essence of sin: 'all have sinned and fall short of the glory of God' (*Rom. 3:23*).

The Book of Daniel gives an account of a king named Belshazzar who was in the midst of a drunken orgy one night when suddenly a hand appeared in mid-air and wrote a message on the wall. It was a message from God to a man who had long spurned God and lived for himself. This is the message Daniel communicated to him:

> O king, the Most High God granted sovereignty, grandeur, glory, and majesty to Nebuchadnezzar your father . . . But when his heart was lifted up and his spirit became so proud that he behaved arrogantly, he was deposed from his royal throne, and his glory was taken away from him . . . until he recognized that the Most High God is ruler over the realm of mankind, and that He sets over it whomever He wishes. Yet you, his son, Belshazzar, have not humbled your heart, even though you knew all this, but you have exalted yourself against the Lord of heaven . . . and you have praised the gods of silver and gold, of bronze, iron, wood and stone, which do not see, hear or understand. But the God in whose hand are your life-breath and your ways, *you have not glorified* (*Dan. 5:18, 20–23*).

The ultimate indictment against Belshazzar is not his impurity, his drunkenness, his gluttony, or his greed. While these things are sinful, they are the fruits of the root of his sin: his attitude of self-dependence, self-seeking, and self-exaltation; in a word, his pride. He refused to humble his heart before the God who had given him breath, and would not live for his glory.

How are men to live for the glory of God? Only by doing the will of God revealed in the Ten Commandments. God is a moral being, who demands that his creatures fulfil their purpose by living a certain kind of life. We are morally accountable to God for the way we live. One day we must give such an account to God.

The Lord Jesus told a parable about a very wealthy man who was consumed with the desire to accumulate so that he might have great security and thereby be free to pursue a life of pleasure:

> And He told them a parable saying, The land of a certain rich man was very productive. And he began reasoning to himself, saying, 'What shall I do, since I have no place to store my crops?' And he said, 'This is what I will do: I will tear down my barns and build larger ones, and there I will store all my grain and my goods. And I will say to my soul, "Soul, you have many goods laid up for many years to come; take your ease, eat, drink, and be merry".' But God said to him, 'You fool! This very night your soul is required of you; and now who will own what you have prepared?' (*Lk. 12:16–20*).

The Bible does not record that this man was an immoral man or a drunkard or a thief. And yet he was a sinner. He failed to reckon with his ultimate accountability to God. His whole life revolved around himself. He did not live for the glory of God. He lived for himself. His god was not the God who created him. His god was materialism. Finally the hour came when those terrible words were spoken by God himself: 'You fool, this very night your soul is required of you.' A day of reckoning came for the man in Jesus' parable, as it will surely come for all of us. Indeed, 'every careless word that men shall speak, they shall render account for it in the day of judgment' (*Matt. 12:36*). There is a day of judgment and all men are morally accountable to God their Creator.

The greatest and most important of all the commandments is the first commandment: 'I am the Lord your God . . . You shall have no other gods before Me' (*Ex. 20:2–3*). Thus, when Jesus was asked which was the greatest of all the commandments he said: 'You shall love the Lord your God with all your heart, and with all your soul, and with all your mind' (*Matt. 22:37*). We can sum up these two commandments by saying: God is to be the centre of life. There are to be no other gods. To have anything in my heart and life which I love more than God or which displaces him, so that I live for that person or thing rather than for him, is idolatry. The Law of God is stating that the foundational principle for the will of God being accomplished in our life is that God must have his rightful place in our hearts.

In 1 John 3:4 we are given a definition of sin: *sin is lawlessness*. Lawlessness means displacing God's will with our own will. Sin is selfishness: God does not rule and direct the life – self does; God is not the centre of the life – self is. Instead of living to fulfil the Creator's will and to glorify him, we live instead to fulfil our own wills and to glorify ourselves. We turn away from God as Lord of our lives, and go our own way.

When our basic attitude towards God is one of rebellion, or self-will and self-pleasing, the result is specific acts of behaviour which transgress his Law. But sin involves not only what we do outwardly; it includes our motives, attitudes, and thoughts; in other words, what we are inwardly. For example, the Lord Jesus tells us that if a man even looks on a woman to lust for her in his heart, in God's eyes he has committed adultery (*Matt. 5:28*); and if a man is angry with another person he commits murder (*Matt. 5:21–22*).

Because men have displaced God from their hearts so that the bent of their lives is self-will, all that can flow out of their lives is selfish actions, thoughts, motives, attitudes, and speech. Because the fountain is polluted at its source, everything that flows from it is polluted. Consequently men's lives become dominated by such sins as the following:

> Anger, jealousy, envy, impure thoughts and actions, impure stories and jokes, cursing, hatred, bigotry, pride, lying, selfish ambitions, stealing, greed, drunkenness, covetousness, love of money, self-exaltation, self-promotion, unforgiveness, bitterness, resentment, impatience, immorality, adultery, homosexuality, violence, murder, rebellion against authority, seeking the praise of men, unkindness, cruelty, arrogance, malice, slander, gossip . . . (*Gal. 5:19–21, 1 Cor. 6:9–10, Rom. 1:18–32, Eph. 5:3–6*).

Of course we could extend this list. But the point is this: because a man's fundamental relationship to God is wrong – because he *is* ungodly – then all of his *behaviour* is unrighteous. Man's whole being, apart from Jesus Christ, is governed by selfishness.

J. I. Packer clearly defines the nature of sin when he writes:

> The words which our Bibles translate as 'sin', in both Old and New Testaments, mean either failing to hit a target or reach a standard, or failing to obey authority. And the standard unreached, the target missed, the path abandoned, the law transgressed, the authority defied, are in each case God's. God and his will are the measure of sin. Sin is turning out of the way he has commanded (Ex. 32:8) into a forbidden way of our own (Isa. 53:6). Sin is going contrary to God, retreating from God, turning one's back on God, defying God, ignoring God.
>
> What, in positive terms, is the essence of sin? *Playing God*, and, as a means to this, refusing to allow the Creator to be God so far as you are concerned. Living, not for him, but for yourself; loving and serving and pleasing yourself without reference to the Creator, trying to be as far as possible independent of him, taking yourself out of his hands, holding him at arm's length, keeping the reins of life in your own hands; acting as if you, and your pleasure, were the end to which all things else, God included, must

> be made to function as a means – that is the attitude in which sin essentially consists.
>
> Sin is exalting oneself against the Creator, withholding the homage due to him, and putting oneself in his place, as the ultimate standard of reference in all life's decisions . . . (*God's Words*, 1981, pp. 72–74).

The Bible makes it very clear that *all* men and women are sinners. We have all turned from God to live for ourselves: '*All* of us like sheep have gone astray, each of us has turned to *his own way*' (*Is. 53:6*); '*All* have sinned and fall short of the *glory* of God' (*Rom. 3:23*). Scripture sums up the condition of men before God in this way: 'There is none righteous, not even one; there is none who understands, there is none who seeks for God; all have turned aside, together they have become useless; there is none who does good, there is not even one' (*Rom. 3:10–12*). This is God's assessment of the entire human race. There is not one righteous person in it; there is no one who is good. We *all* have sinned by transgressing God's laws and by refusing him his rightful place in our lives.

No one can stand before God and say, 'I am a holy person' or 'I am a righteous person', because God demands *perfect* obedience. God is holy and absolutely pure in his moral character and he cannot accept anyone into his presence who is not perfectly holy. To be perfect means that an individual has to keep the Law of God in its entirety in thought and deed and never transgress it at any point in his life. All of us are accountable to him to keep his Law perfectly. Not to do so is to sin and incur eternal judgment: 'For as many as are of the works of the Law are under a curse; for it is written, "Cursed is everyone who does not abide by all things written in the book of the law to perform them"' (*Gal. 3:10*).

The Law of God holds all men accountable to obey it; but there is no one who can stand before God on the basis of the Law and be justified before him. It demands a perfect obedience, but it was never given to be a means by which an individual might save himself. Rather it was given as a standard which reveals sin, and shows us how far short we fall in doing the will of God in our thoughts, motives, attitudes, speech, and actions. Romans 3:20 reveals this purpose to us: 'Because by the works of the Law no flesh will be justified in His sight; for *through the Law comes the knowledge of sin*.' The Law of God shows a man that he is a sinner, by revealing a standard which he has disobeyed, and showing him that he has not fulfilled the purpose for which he was created.

The Bible further teaches us that because our God is a holy God, he is also a God of wrath. That is, he is a God who will judge sin: 'For the *wrath* of God is revealed from heaven against all ungodliness and unrighteousness of men, who suppress the truth in unrighteousness' (*Rom. 1:18*). Scripture says that 'He is angry with the wicked every day' (*Ps. 7:11*). God's wrath is manifested against us because of our unrighteous behaviour. We have transgressed his holy Law. We have not loved him with all our hearts; we have not sought to obey his will above all else. We have served other gods before him. We are guilty. And the penalty for transgressing the Law of God is eternal death: 'The soul that sins, it shall *die*' (*Ezek. 18:4*); 'The wages of sin is *death*' (*Rom. 6:23*). We have rebelled and therefore face eternal judgment and condemnation in hell.

Hell is a real place – a place of judgment and condemnation for sin which lasts for eternity. Revelation 20:11–15 gives us a clear description of the judgment of God upon those who die in their sins, and the nature of their eternal destiny:

> And I saw a great white throne and Him who sat upon it, from whose presence earth and heaven fled away, and no place was found for them. And I saw the dead, the great and the small, standing before the throne, and books were opened; and another book was opened, which is the book of life; and the dead were judged from the things which were

> written in the books, according to their deeds. And the sea gave up the dead which were in it, and death and Hades gave up the dead which were in them; and they were judged, every one of them according to their deeds. And death and Hades were thrown into the lake of fire. This is the second death, the lake of fire. And if anyone's name was not found written in the book of life, he was thrown into the lake of fire.

There are two types of people here: those who are judged and eternally condemned in the lake of fire, and those who escape judgment because their names are written in the book of life. Those who are judged and condemned are judged according to their deeds and their behaviour. Their lives are compared to the demands of the Law of God and they are found guilty and condemned. This judgment of God is very real. The Bible tells us that 'it is appointed for men to die once and after this comes judgment' (*Heb. 9:27*). But the wonderful news of the gospel is that it is possible to escape the judgment of God. It is possible to have one's name written in the Lamb's 'book of life', and so be saved, forgiven, and delivered from guilt and condemnation, from the power of sin, and from an eternal hell. It is possible to receive a new life in which we are reconciled to God and enabled to live for his glory. This is what the Lord Jesus came to accomplish: 'For the Son of Man has come to seek and to save that which was lost' (*Lk. 19:10*).

Jesus is the Saviour. He alone can deal with our sins. Apart from him we have absolutely no hope. For, if I have to be perfect in order to get to heaven and stand before God, I am doomed. I have no hope. I *must* have a saviour. That is exactly what the Lord Jesus has come to be. But apart from him there is no salvation. If a man dies in his sins apart from Jesus Christ, then that man will spend eternity in hell under the wrath of God: 'He who believes in the Son has eternal life; but he who does not obey the Son shall not see life, but the wrath of God abides on him' (*Jn. 3:36*).

We are accountable to God to keep his Law perfectly. If we fail to obey him perfectly, then he will judge sin; every soul that sins shall die eternally. But because God is also a God of love he takes no pleasure in the death of the wicked, and therefore has provided a Saviour in his Son, the Lord Jesus Christ. Through him we can find salvation and deliverance from sin and guilt and eternal hell.

9: *The Work of Jesus Christ*

The Law of God, the Bible says, is righteous, holy, and just. It is an expression of the character of God himself. Because of the nature of God, as just and holy, the demands of his Law *must* be fulfilled. Sin *must* be judged. The penalty *must* be paid. God's wrath and judgment *must* be poured out on sin. That means he must judge the sinner (we cannot separate sin from the sinner). Yet, God is a God of love who desires to forgive men. How is God to be true to his Law, which he cannot compromise, and yet be able to forgive our sins and accept us?

There are two things which the Law of God demands:

1. A perfect life if we are to be able to stand before him. In order to go to heaven we must be perfect.
2. Eternal judgment and condemnation for those who disobey it.

This is where the gospel comes in. The gospel is the good news that God himself has fulfilled the demands of the Law on our behalf; he can now forgive us and accept us in Jesus Christ. He can be just and at the same time justify guilty sinners. We can escape eternal judgment and condemnation because Jesus Christ has fulfilled the Law of God *for* us.

How can this be? The Lord Jesus came to this earth as a man to be our substitute, in order to fulfil the requirements of the Law of God on our behalf and to free us from its curse: 'But when the fulness of the time came, God sent forth His Son, born of a woman, born under the Law, in order that He might redeem those who were under the Law, that we might receive the adoption as sons' (*Gal. 4:4*). Christ was born as a man under the Law. He was subject to its authority and its demands, and has fulfilled that Law in every detail as our substitute, as a Representative Man, and can therefore be our Saviour. How has he done this?

First of all, Christ came as a man in order to pay the penalty for our sins: the penalty of death. Jesus came to die: 'For even the Son of Man did not come to be served, but to serve, and to give His life a ransom for many' (*Mk. 10:45*). Thus, he 'redeemed us from the curse of the Law, having become a curse *for* us – for it is written, Cursed is everyone who hangs on a tree' (*Gal. 3:13*). When Paul says Jesus became a curse he means that he took our guilt and then received the righteous judgment of God against sin in his own body on the cross. He bore *our* judgment in *our* place. He became our substitute. 'He made Him who knew no sin to be sin on our behalf . . .' (*2 Cor. 5:21*).

In Hebrews 2:14,15,17 we are told that:

> Since then the children share in flesh and blood, He Himself likewise also partook of the same, that through death He might render powerless him who had the power of death, that is, the devil; and might deliver those who through fear of death were subject to slavery all their lives . . . Therefore, He had to be made like His brethren in all things, that He might become a merciful and faithful high priest in things pertaining to God, to make *propitiation* for the sins of the people.

'Propitiation' (used here and also in *Rom. 3:25, 1 Jn. 2:2*) is a very important word. As we mentioned in chapter four it means the satisfying of wrath. The Lord Jesus went to the cross to bear the wrath of God for our sin in his own body. God's own Son was slain in our place, in order that he might then rise again to offer us forgiveness and salvation.

God's Law is an expression of his holiness. He cannot simply forgive and show mercy and forget about the Law. To do so would be to compromise his holiness. He cannot exercise his love at the expense of his holiness, righteousness, and justice. Therefore the Father and the Son together planned salvation in such a way that God remains just and at the same time forgives men their transgressions, by providing a substitute who will take man's place.

There is a graphic and poignant illustration of this in the Old Testament in the story of Abraham and Isaac. God commanded Abraham to take his only son, Isaac, whom he dearly loved, the son God had *promised*, and to offer him as a burnt offering at a specific place God would designate. Imagine Abraham's agony of heart! But he obeyed God. He and Isaac went together to the mountain that God showed him. The biblical account pictures the father and son walking along together. The son is meek and submissive, the father very determined: 'And Abraham took the wood of the burnt offering and laid it on Isaac his son, and he took in his hand the fire and the knife. So the two of them walked on together' (*Gen. 22:6*). On his back, Isaac carried the wood upon which he was to be sacrificed, while Abraham carried the fire and the knife.

This story points forward to another *promised* Son who would carry on his back a wooden cross on which he would be sacrificed. Abraham carried the fire to consume his son, and the knife to slay him. The sacrificial fire reminds us of the wrath of God which was to consume his Son, as he offered himself as a propitiation for the sins of the world. Surpassing his own command to Abraham, God 'did not spare His own Son, but delivered Him up for us all . . .' (*Rom. 8:32*). The death of Jesus was no accident. It was planned, initiated, and completed by God himself. It was predicted and foretold in the Old Testament long before it happened. But this picture of Abraham and Isaac helps us to understand that it is not some cold, impersonal thing that has happened. This is a Father pouring out his wrath on the Son he dearly loves so that the just demands of his Law might be fulfilled in order to save us. This incident helps us to understand, in some limited way, what it cost the Father to provide salvation for us.

It is immensely interesting to note where it was that God told Abraham to go to offer up Isaac – Mount Moriah. It is mentioned again in 2 Chronicles 3:1: 'Then Solomon began to build the house of the Lord in Jerusalem on Mount Moriah, where the Lord had appeared to his father David . . .'. This mountain where Abraham offered up Isaac was later to become the location of the Temple sacrifices in the Temple at Jerusalem. In the fullness of time, on that very same mountain, at a place called Calvary, God the Father gave up his only Son as an atoning sacrifice for the sins of the world. In that place, all that was illustrated in Isaac and those countless animal sacrifices was fulfilled in terrible reality.

The Lord Jesus Christ has taken our sins to himself, and has gone to the cross as our substitute, to suffer and endure the judgment and condemnation of God against them: 'He Himself bore *our sins* in His body on the cross' (*1 Pet. 2:24*); 'He was pierced through for *our transgressions*, He was crushed for *our iniquities*; the chastening for our well-being fell upon Him, and by His scourging we are healed . . . the Lord has caused the iniquity of us all to fall on Him' (*Is. 53:5–6*). The shedding of his blood has made an atonement for our sin and his sacrifice has completely satisfied the righteous requirements of the Law of God. The payment has been made.

This principle of a substitutionary atonement effected through the shedding of blood was established very early in Israel's history when God first brought the sacrificial system into being: 'For the life of the flesh is in the blood, and I have given it to you on the altar to make an atonement for your souls; for it is the blood by reason of the life that makes atonement' (*Lev. 17:11*). God was teaching his people the principle that sin must be judged, and that the Law demands death for sin. The Old Testament sacrificial system provided a temporary solution for the sins of the people. An animal could be sacrificed in their place and the guilt of their sin temporarily covered until One would come to make the ultimate substitutionary atonement. Thus, the Lord Jesus was declared by John the Baptist to be 'the Lamb of God who takes away the sin of the world' (*Jn. 1:29*).

In Jesus Christ the demands of the Law of God have been fulfilled. By faith a Christian is united to Christ and is therefore 'in Him'; he is identified with Jesus in his death, burial, and resurrection. Thus, when Jesus Christ died on the cross, the Christian also died; in Christ, the penalty of the Law of God against him has been already fully administered. This is why the Bible says, 'There is therefore now no condemnation for those who are in Christ Jesus' (*Rom. 8:1*). The Christian is now completely set free, completely forgiven; all his or her sins have been dealt with. God will not condemn me if I am in his Son, for he judged his Son as my substitute. God has taken my sins away and he remembers them no more. He completely forgets them.

But God's Law also demands perfect obedience if we are going to be able to stand before him. God is perfectly holy. Since nothing sinful can stand in his presence, *we have to be perfect to go to heaven*. How did Jesus fulfil *this* requirement of the Law of God on our behalf? As we have seen, the Lord Jesus Christ was born of a woman under the Law of God. He was subject to the authority of that Law, and as a man he kept the Law of God perfectly. He committed no sin (*1 Pet. 2:22*). The perfect life that we are required to live, he has lived. Jesus' life was lived solely to the glory of God. He was a perfect man; he never violated the Law of God. It is his perfection and his righteousness which God will give to those who come by repentance and faith to Jesus Christ. The very perfection we need in order to stand before God has been lived out for us by Jesus Christ and is available to us as a gift to be received by faith. Paul puts it like this:

> More than that, I count all things to be loss in view of the surpassing value of knowing Christ Jesus my Lord, for whom I have suffered the loss of all things, and count them but rubbish in order that I may gain Christ, and may be found in Him, not having a righteousness of my own derived from the Law, but that which is through faith in Christ, the righteousness which comes from God on the basis of faith (*Phil. 3:8–9*).

This does not mean that we are already perfect! We are *declared* to be righteous. This is what the Bible means by justification. Our sins are forgiven and we are also given a positive righteousness so that we can be fully and finally accepted by God. Unfortunately it is here that so many Roman Catholics stumble. They are very similar to the Jews Paul describes in Romans 10:1–4: 'Brethren, my heart's desire and my prayer to God for them is for their salvation. For I bear them witness that they have a zeal for God, but not in accordance with knowledge. For not knowing about God's righteousness, and seeking to establish their own, they did not subject themselves to the righteousness of God. For Christ is the end of the law for righteousness to everyone who believes.'

These Jews were zealous but they were sadly mistaken about God's way of salvation. His way is not the way of works. Righteousness is received as a gift by faith.

SUMMARY

The Lord Jesus Christ has perfectly fulfilled the demands of God's Law to which every one of us is accountable. The Law demands death for the transgressor. Jesus fulfilled that demand on the cross. The Law demands a perfect obedience if we are to be accepted by God. Jesus lived a perfect life under the Law of God, and fulfilled that demand on our behalf. The whole of our salvation is, therefore, found in Christ. His work in fulfilling the Law of God for us, as our substitute, secures for us an *eternal* salvation which can never be lost.

This is why Jesus says that he alone is 'the way, and the truth, and the life', the only way to God (*Jn. 14:6*); and why Peter says that 'there is salvation in no one else; for there is no other name under heaven that has been given among men, by which we must be saved' (*Acts 4:12*). No one else can fulfil the requirements of the Law of God and at the same time deal with our sins and give us a positive righteousness to stand before God. No other person or religion can fulfil the Law of God on our behalf. Salvation comes to us on the basis of the sacrifice and righteousness of Jesus Christ alone – a theme which has been echoed and re-echoed throughout the church among those who are true Christians.

Jesus, Thy blood and righteousness
My beauty are, my glorious dress;
'Midst flaming worlds, in these arrayed,
With joy shall I lift up my head.
Count Zinzendorf

Not the labours of my hands
Can fulfil Thy law's demands;
Could my zeal no respite know,
Could my tears for ever flow,
All for sin could not atone;
Thou must save, and Thou alone.

Nothing in my hand I bring,
Simply to Thy cross I cling;
Naked, come to Thee for dress;
Helpless, look to Thee for grace;
Foul, I to the fountain fly;
Wash me, Saviour, or I die.
A. M. Toplady

Once I know these facts and realise that there is a complete salvation provided by God, the next question I must ask is this: how do I get that salvation? How can this become real in my life?

In his Word, God gives us very specific instructions about the means by which that salvation is appropriated. It is by repentance and faith. This is the theme of our next chapter.

10: *Repentance and Faith*

We have come to the point in this study of asking the question which the Philippian jailer asked the apostle Paul, 'What must I do to be saved?' (*Acts 16:30*). *How* does salvation become ours? How can we experience forgiveness of sins and acceptance with God, be adopted into his family, and receive the gift of eternal life? Just because the Lord Jesus Christ has done the work of salvation does not mean that every person is automatically saved. The Bible clearly tells us there are certain conditions which must be fulfilled if the work of Jesus Christ is to be applied to our lives.

First of all we need to understand that God never gives salvation to us apart from the Lord Jesus Christ himself. Salvation becomes ours only when we become rightly related to Jesus Christ as a person; that is, when we come to know him. Christ himself said: 'This is eternal life, that they may know Thee the only true God, and Jesus Christ whom Thou hast sent' (*Jn. 17:3*).

Salvation is not membership in a church, or merely intellectual assent to certain biblical doctrines. It is not a matter of partaking of sacraments or rituals or striving to live up to a certain moral ethic. Salvation involves coming into a living, personal relationship with Jesus Christ.

In the Gospels it is clear that Jesus Christ called men to come to him directly, apart from any human mediation. He said, for example, 'Come to *Me*, all who are weary and heavy laden, and I will give you rest. Take My yoke upon you, and learn from *Me*, for I am gentle and humble in heart;

and you shall find rest for your souls' (*Matt. 11:28–29*); 'I am the bread of life; he who *comes to Me* shall not hunger, and he who *believes in Me* shall never thirst' (*Jn. 6:35*). John comments: 'But as many as *received Him*, to them He gave the right to become children of God, even to those who believe in His name' (*Jn. 1:12*).

Eternal life is received by coming directly and personally to Jesus Christ himself. By contrast, the Roman Catholic Church teaches that *it* is the 'universal sacrament of salvation'. It teaches that if someone becomes a member of that Church and participates in the sacraments, then that person is a Christian. It claims to be the means whereby the grace of God and the merits of Jesus are channelled to the individual through the sacraments, and that people are saved by their relation to the Church, rather than to Jesus himself. Individuals then trust in the Church and its ritual and sacraments for salvation rather than in Jesus Christ. We have already seen that the Roman Church's whole teaching on the Mass, the Priesthood, the Eucharist, Confession, and Baptism is completely contrary to the teaching of the Word of God. Thus Christ is displaced by a false gospel.

Once we see that we can come to Jesus personally and directly, the next question to answer is: *how* do I come to him?

The Bible tells us there are two conditions which must be met if a person is to *know* Jesus Christ and be saved:

1. He must repent.
2. He must believe.

The New Testament frequently emphasises this. For example in Mark 1:15 the Lord Jesus states: 'The time is fulfilled, and the kingdom of God is at hand; *repent and believe* in the gospel.' In Luke 13:3, he says, 'Unless you *repent*, you will all likewise perish.' In Luke 5:32, he says he came 'to call sinners to *repentance*'.

The Lord Jesus Christ, John the Baptist, Peter, and Paul all preached repentance as a necessary condition for salvation. In the same way, faith is emphasised as a necessary condition for salvation: 'For God so loved the world, that He gave His only begotten Son, that whoever *believes* in Him should not perish, but have eternal life' (*Jn. 3:16*). Again, Paul states, 'By grace you have been saved through *faith* . . .' (*Eph. 2:8*).

What do we mean by repentance and faith? Repentance and faith are two sides of the same coin. Dr Augustus Strong writes:

> Repentance is that voluntary change in the mind of the sinner in which he *turns from* sin. Being essentially a change of mind, it involves a change of view, a change of feeling and a change of purpose . . . Faith is that voluntary change in the mind of the sinner in which he *turns to* Christ . . . The voluntary element is trust in Christ as Lord and Savior, or to distinguish its two aspects: a) surrender of the soul as guilty and defiled to Christ's governance, b) reception and appropriation of Christ as the source of pardon and spiritual life (*Systematic Theology*, pp. 829, 832–36).

The essential thought in repentance and faith is that of turning. Repentance is turning *from* sin while faith is turning *to* Christ. The result is self-surrender and trust in Jesus Christ as Lord and Saviour. The guilty sinner turns from all sin, yields his will to Jesus Christ, and trusts in him as his Saviour.

In Philippians chapter 3, the apostle Paul describes what this involved in his own life. He lists his credentials: 'If anyone else has a mind to put confidence in the flesh, I far more . . .'. If there was ever a man who, from a human perspective, could stand before God because of what he was and had done, it was Paul. He lists his achievements: his heredity, his position in society, and his zealous works:

'Circumcised the eighth day, of the nation of Israel, of the tribe of Benjamin, a Hebrew of Hebrews, as to the Law, a Pharisee; as to zeal, a persecutor of the church, as to the righteousness which is in the Law, found blameless' (*Phil. 3:5–6*).

At one time Paul had a very high estimate of himself. From a human perspective, no one could match Paul for zeal, for morality, for purity of heredity or religious observance. And yet he tells us what became of his estimate of those things when he came to know Jesus Christ: 'But whatever things were gain to me, those things I have counted as *loss* for the sake of Christ. More than that, I count all things to be loss in view of the surpassing value of knowing Christ Jesus my Lord, for whom I have suffered the loss of all things, and *count them but rubbish* in order that I may gain Christ, and may be found in Him, not having a righteousness of my own derived from the Law, but that which is through faith in Christ, the righteousness which comes from God on the basis of faith' (*Phil. 3:7–9*).

Paul had to come to the point where he saw that all his achievements and good works were worthless in God's eyes, and that he was nothing more than a bankrupt sinner with a proud heart. He therefore had to turn from all his good works and his high estimate of himself. He came to Jesus Christ with empty hands, to cast himself on his mercy and to receive salvation. He himself had not achieved it. It had been achieved *for* him. He therefore abandoned any attempt to save himself, and trusted completely in Jesus Christ. In other words, he turned *from* self-righteousness *to* Jesus as Saviour. In so turning he received the perfect righteousness of Jesus as a gift.

This salvation cannot be earned. It cannot be merited by human works. It must be received as a gift of God based solely upon his mercy and grace: 'To the one *who does not work*, but believes in Him who justifies the ungodly, his *faith* is reckoned as righteousness' (*Rom. 4:5*).

This does not discount the importance of living a holy life. The person who truly becomes a Christian *will* live a holy life, for salvation involves the reversing of this way of living. It is not only deliverance from the guilt of sin but also from the power of sin. It includes sanctification. In salvation we are restored to that original purpose for which we were created, to be under the authority and rule of God, to live for his will and glory.

Repentance therefore is turning from sin. It is turning from self-will and forsaking everything on this earth which is opposed to God and his will, in order to know and do the will of God, for his glory.

When the rich young ruler came to Jesus, he fell at his feet and earnestly implored him to explain what he needed to do to inherit eternal life. He was morally upright and sincere. When Jesus quoted the Law of God, the young man claimed to have kept it from the time of his youth. But then Jesus uttered these devastating words to him: '"One thing you lack: go and sell all you possess, and give to the poor, and you shall have treasure in heaven; and come, follow Me." But at these words his face fell, and he went away grieved, for he was one who owned much property' (*Mk. 10:21–22*).

What had Jesus done? He had put his finger on the man's idol and shown him that he had another god – material possessions – instead of the one true and living God. Thus, Jesus had shown him that he had broken the first and most important of all the commandments: 'I am the Lord your God . . . you shall have no other gods before Me.'

If he were to receive eternal life that idol must be dethroned and forsaken, and God must be given his rightful place. Therefore Jesus told him to forsake all his riches and to come and follow him. This was simply the application of a general principle. If any man is to come to Jesus, then Jesus must be Lord of all to him.

In summing up the gospel he preached, the apostle Paul said that he preached 'repentance toward God and faith in our Lord Jesus Christ' (*Acts 20:21*). Unless a man repents towards God he cannot savingly believe in Jesus Christ. True repentance is a change of mind towards God. It is yielding one's will to Christ's control and coming under his authority. Self no longer rules, Christ does.

Have you yielded your will to Christ and given him absolute control of your life? Is he your Lord? Have you turned from living for yourself and the world and all it offers in terms of possessions and pleasure and position, to live solely for Jesus Christ and the kingdom of God?

Is Jesus alone your Saviour? Or are you trusting in something else, or in addition, for acceptance with God? Are you trusting in a church, in your good works, or in the sacraments? Are you trusting in your own goodness and sincerity? Have you forsaken every form of works, be they religious or moral, and cast yourself totally by faith upon Jesus alone to save you? Have you come to him and received salvation as a gift by faith?

11: *The Results of Salvation*

'Salvation' in the Word of God is a very broad concept. To many the word 'salvation' means little more than deliverance from hell. But salvation means much more than this and it can be summed up under three major headings:

1. Justification
2. Sanctification
3. Glorification

Each of these blessings becomes ours when Jesus Christ is our Lord and Saviour.

JUSTIFICATION

As we have already noted, 'to be justified' is a legal term which means 'to be declared righteous'. When God unites us to Jesus Christ we are acquitted from condemnation under the Law of God, and the righteousness of Christ is credited to our account.

Justification brings peace with God: 'Therefore having been justified by faith, we have peace with God through our Lord Jesus Christ' (*Rom. 5:1*). Our guilt is gone. God's enmity has been dealt with in Christ; now there is peace with God.

Justification takes place the moment we are united to Jesus Christ, and it is permanent. Since the basis for it is the work of Jesus Christ we can never lose it. A true Christian's standing before God can *never change* because the demands of the Law have all been fulfilled.

But our salvation does not stop at justification.

SANCTIFICATION

To sanctify means to set apart. Sanctification, in Scripture, means to be set apart to God for his purposes. This is why Jesus Christ gave himself on the cross for us: 'He died for all, that they who live should *no longer live for themselves, but for Him* who died and rose again on their behalf' (*2 Cor. 5:15*). In essence this sums up sanctification: no longer to live for self but for him who died and rose again for us.

We live for him by living for his will revealed in the Word of God. The Bible tells us that those who know God are those who keep his commandments: 'And by this we know that we have come to know Him, if we keep His commandments. The one who says, "I have come to know Him," and does not keep His commandments, is a liar, and the truth is not in him' (*1 Jn. 2:3–4*).

Whereas we used to live for ourselves, we now live for Jesus Christ. Where we used to live for this world and the fulfilment of our own interests and ambitions, we now live for the kingdom of God and the fulfilment of *his* interests. Where we used to live in specific sins, we now strive to be holy.

Again, the purpose of salvation and the work of Jesus Christ on the cross was to restore us to fellowship with God, so that the original purpose for which we were created – to fulfil the Law of God – might be accomplished. 'For what the Law could not do, weak as it was through the flesh, God did: sending His own Son in the likeness of sinful flesh and as an offering for sin, He condemned sin in the flesh, *in order that the requirement of the Law might be fulfilled in us*, who do not walk according to the flesh, but according to the Spirit' (*Rom. 8:3–4*).

We were created to do the will of God. When God recreates

us spiritually through the new birth his purpose is fulfilled. He makes us holy. 'For the grace of God has appeared, bringing salvation to all men, instructing us to deny ungodliness and worldly desires and to live sensibly, righteously and godly in the present age, looking for the blessed hope and the appearing of the glory of our great God and Savior, Christ Jesus; who gave Himself for us, that He might redeem us from every lawless deed and purify for Himself a people for His own possession, zealous for good deeds' (*Tit. 2:11–14*).

The evidence of faith in Christ is a life of new obedience to God. The Lord Jesus tells us this in unmistakable terms: 'Not everyone who says to Me, "Lord, Lord," will enter the kingdom of heaven; but *he who does the will of My Father*, who is in heaven. Many will say to Me on that day, "Lord, Lord, did we not prophesy in Your name, and in Your name cast out demons, and in Your name perform many miracles?" And then I will declare to them, "I never knew you; depart from Me, you who practice lawlessness"' (*Matt. 7:21–24*). It is not those who *say* 'Lord Lord', but those who do the will of God who will enter heaven. It is not those who *say* that he is Lord who are Christ's disciples, but those who *submit* to him as Lord and no longer live for self but for the will of God. Only the one who does the will of God abides forever (*1 Jn. 2:17*). Though these people professed Jesus Christ, and acknowledged him to be Lord, and were even active in ministry in his name, they lived fundamentally for themselves while they professed Jesus Christ. The sad truth is that they were lost. They had never truly repented.

When we truly come to know Jesus Christ, our life is transformed. It becomes a sanctified life. Jesus Christ himself dwells in our hearts, by his Spirit. When we say that someone is 'sanctified' or 'holy', we are saying that he or she is becoming more like Jesus Christ. The life of Christ himself becomes manifested in such a person's life. This is what Paul means when he says: 'I have been crucified with

Christ; and it is no longer I who live, but Christ lives in me; and the life which I now live in the flesh I live by faith in the Son of God, who loved me, and delivered Himself up for me' (*Gal. 2:20*). Again, he says in 2 Corinthians 5:17: 'If any man is in Christ, he is a new creature; the old things passed away; behold, new things have come.'

If Christianity means sharing in the life of Christ, what was his life like?

1. The life of Jesus was first and foremost a life totally committed to the will of God. He did not live to please himself: 'For I have come down from heaven, not to do My own will, but the will of Him who sent Me' (*Jn. 6:38*); 'For even Christ did not please Himself' (*Rom. 15:3*).
2. His life was one of absolute dependence upon God for all things. It was a life of faith: 'Truly, truly, I say to you, the Son can do nothing of Himself . . . I can do nothing on My own initiative' (*Jn. 5:19,30*). His life was lived in total dependence on the Spirit of God (*Lk. 4:1,14,18*).
3. Jesus' great desire was for God to be glorified in his life regardless of the cost to himself: 'Now My soul has become troubled; and what shall I say, "Father, save Me from this hour?" But for this purpose I came to this hour. Father, glorify Thy name' (*Jn. 12:27–28*).
4. He was a man who kept God's Word and who loved holiness. He did only those things that pleased his Father: 'Man shall not live on bread alone, but on every word that proceeds out of the mouth of God' (*Matt. 4:4*); 'I always do the things that are pleasing to Him' (*Jn. 8:29*); 'I do know Him, and keep His Word' (*Jn. 8:55*).
5. Jesus' life was one of intimate personal communion with God. God was a living reality to him. He spoke of God in the most intimate of terms, calling him *Abba*, Father. He said, 'I know Him' (*Jn. 8:55*).

6. His life was a life of prayer: 'And in the early morning, while it was still dark, He arose and went out and departed to a lonely place, and was praying there' (*Mk. 1:35*).
7. He had a servant spirit: 'For even the Son of Man did not come to be served, but to serve, and to give His life a ransom for many' (*Mk. 10:45*).
8. His life was characterised by love. He lived for the sake of others: 'A new commandment I give to you, that you love one another, *even as I have loved you*, that you also love one another' (*Jn. 13:34*).
9. In being absolutely committed to the will of God, Jesus never turned aside as a result of persecution, trial, or suffering. He endured and persevered in the face of the most difficult circumstances. Nothing could deter him from fulfilling the will of God, even though to live such a life meant rejection by his family, his countrymen, the religious leaders, betrayal by his disciples, and ultimately torture and death: he 'for the joy set before Him endured the cross, despising the shame, and has sat down at the right hand of the throne of God. For consider Him who has endured such hostility by sinners against Himself, so that you may not grow weary and lose heart' (*Heb. 12:2–3*).
10. The Lord Jesus himself tells us what he is like. He said, 'I am gentle and humble in heart' (*Matt. 11:29*). He did not live to promote himself. He was not trying to be 'somebody' in the eyes of men. He did not live for the glory, approval, acceptance, or praise of men. He was God's servant. And as God's servant he was a man under authority. Frequently the Lord Jesus referred to himself as being 'sent': 'For I have come down from heaven, not to do My own will, but the will of *Him who sent Me*' (*Jn. 6:38;* cf. *5:36; 7:29; 8:42;* etc.).
11. Finally Jesus' life was characterised by devotion to the kingdom of God. He did not live for this world. He lived in order that the kingdom of God would come into the hearts

> of men. He had a passion that men would come to know and glorify God in their lives. He sought '*first* the kingdom of God and His righteousness' (*Matt. 6:33*). Jesus said: 'My food is to do the will of Him who sent Me, and to accomplish His work. Do you not say, "There are yet four months, and then comes the harvest"? Behold, I say to you, lift up your eyes, and look on the fields, that they are white for harvest' (*Jn. 4:34–35*).

The life of Jesus Christ was *dominated* by God and his interests. God was not just a convenient addition to his life; God *was* his life. The same will be true of those who truly know him. This kind of life will not be lived perfectly but it certainly is going to be the *bent* of a person's life. And the older we grow in our relationship with Christ, the more we will become like him.

It is not what we profess but how we live which *proves* whether or not our faith is genuine. When we respond properly to the gospel through repentance and faith, we are not only forgiven, made right with God, and brought into his family, but also set apart unto God for *his* purposes, and our life begins to be sanctified.

When I was a Roman Catholic I used to go to confession on a weekly basis and do all the required penance. But week after week I came back with the same sins. I secretly held the notion that I could go on committing those sins. All I had to do was go to confession, do the required penance, and then everything would be fine. That is a terrible deception. God does not want penance. He wants repentance. He wants a resolute *forsaking* of all sin and a commitment to Jesus Christ as the Lord, who gives us power to obey God.

Who is the person who has received eternal life? The one whose life is characterised by the fruit of sanctification! Who is the person who is sanctified? The one who has become a servant of God. And who is the person who is a servant of God? The one who has been freed from sin (*Rom. 6:22*).

Sin involves self-will and self-rule. We are freed from self-will only when Jesus Christ is enthroned as Lord, and we thus become enslaved to God. Such 'bondage' is our only true freedom, and the result is a sanctified life which leads to eternal life.

Are you a changed man, a changed woman? Have you received a new heart? Has your life been sanctified to God so that you live for him? Or do you live for yourself? Do you hunger and thirst for righteousness from your heart? Do you long to be holy? Do you spend time alone with God in his Word and prayer? Is your life characterised by prayer? Do you seek him? Is he Lord of your life? Do you live for the kingdom of God? Do you have a passion that men hear the gospel and come into the kingdom of God? Or do you live for this world and the fulfilment of your own desires and interests? *Whom* do you live for? *What* do you live for?

GLORIFICATION

Finally, salvation includes glorification. The person who is united to Christ is assured of glorification one day. We are going to be completely transformed into the likeness of Jesus Christ himself, and we will be perfect in every area of our being. We will have no more sin!

Sanctification is the process whereby we grow more and more into conformity with the character of Jesus Christ. It is a process of development of which glorification is the ultimate fulfilment. It is its culmination. Then we will be *absolutely* conformed to the character of Jesus without any defect of any kind: 'Beloved, now we are children of God, and it has not appeared as yet what we shall be. We know that, when He appears, *we shall be like Him*' (*1 Jn. 3:2*).

To be saved ultimately involves being glorified. We can

never lose our salvation for the Word of God tells us that those God justifies he also glorifies: 'For whom He foreknew, He also predestined to become conformed to the image of His Son, that He might be the first-born among many brethren; and whom He predestined, these He also called; and whom He called, these He also justified; *and whom He justified, these He also glorified*' (*Rom. 8:29–30*). Once we are justified, there is absolutely nothing that can separate us from the love of God. Our eternal destiny is absolutely secure.

What a wonderful salvation our God has provided us in his Son! What more fitting way to conclude this study than by echoing the praises of God in the eighth chapter of Romans. Here Paul gives us his summation of the salvation which we have been considering. Here we learn about *justification*, in which we are set free from all condemnation through the work of Jesus Christ; about *sanctification*, in which we are totally committed to the will of God no matter what the cost. And finally we learn about *glorification* and eternal security where Paul declares that nothing can separate us from the love of God in Christ Jesus!

JUSTIFICATION

> What then shall we say to these things? If God is for us, who is against us? He who did not spare His own Son, but delivered Him up for us all, how will He not also with Him freely give us all things? Who will bring a charge against God's elect? God is the one who justifies; who is the one who condemns? Christ Jesus is He who died, yes, rather who was raised, who is at the right hand of God, who also intercedes for us.

SANCTIFICATION

> Who shall separate us from the love of Christ? Shall tribulation, or distress, or persecution, or famine, or

nakedness, or peril, or sword? Just as it is written, 'For Thy sake we are being put to death all day long; we were considered as sheep to be slaughtered.' But in all these things we overwhelmingly conquer through Him who loved us.

GLORIFICATION

For I am convinced that neither death, nor life, nor angels, nor principalities, nor things present, nor things to come, nor powers, nor height, nor depth, nor any other created thing, shall be able to separate us from the love of God, which is in Christ Jesus our Lord. (*Rom. 8:31–39*)

APPENDICES

Appendix A

OFFICIAL SOURCES OF ROMAN CATHOLIC DOCTRINE

The author expresses his thanks to the following publishers for permisssion to quote from their material:

1. *The Canons and Decrees of the Council of Trent*, in Philip Schaff, *The Creeds of Christendom*, Baker Book House (1919 ed.).
2. *The Documents of Vatican II*, Walter M. Abbott S.J., General Editor, Association Press, Follett Publishing Company, 1966.
3. *The Code of Canon Law*, Prepared by The Canon Law Society of Great Britain and Ireland in association with The Canon Law Society of Australia and New Zealand and the Canadian Canon Law Society, William Collins and William B. Eerdmans Publishing Company, 1983.

John Paul II makes the following comments concerning *The Code of Canon Law*:

> It is hoped that this English version of the Code will be a fitting resource for an attentive and fruitful study of the law of the Church . . .
>
> We order that henceforth it is to have the force of law for the whole latin Church, and we commit its observance to the care and vigilance of all who are responsible.

4. *The Question and Answer Catholic Catechism*, John A. Hardon S.J., Image Books, Doubleday and Company, 1981.

Nihil Obstat: William B. Smith, S.T.D., Censor Librorum. *Imprimatur*: Joseph T. O'Keefe, Vicar General, Archdiocese of New York, July 7, 1981.

John A. Hardon S.J. is a Jesuit scholar who is a professor in the Institute for Advanced Studies in Catholic Doctrine at St. John's University in New York.

The foreword to the Catechism was written by Silvio Cardinal Oddi, Prefect of the Sacred Congregation for the Clergy, Vatican City. Thus this document carries the official authorisation of the Vatican. He makes the following comments:

> Father John A. Hardon . . . after producing a superior work on Catholic doctrine in straight prose, . . . now offers a refreshing treatment of the same matter in question and answer form, thereby offering a genuine service to English-speaking Catholics . . .
>
> Good catechetical style requires precision and brevity. Vague authors, therefore, eschew it, either because their thoughts are muddled or because they are wily enough not to put down what they really hold in black and white.
>
> Father Hardon, who is neither obscure in his theology nor wordy in his presentation, proves himself in this present book to be a master of catechetical pedagogy.
>
> *The Question and Answer Catholic Catechism* could hardly be more timely. Today's Catholics, particularly the most faithful among them, need to know the latest developments in the Church's teaching and, above all, to be reassured that the faith has not changed . . .
>
> It is clear that Father Hardon has striven successfully to expound the authentic teaching of Holy Mother Church. Readers will find in the book an up-to-date, reliable presentation of the same dogmatic, moral, ascetical, and liturgical truths which the Catholic Church has always taught.
>
> Apart from doctrinal fidelity and theological precision, the scope of the book sets it apart from many of its genre.
>
> The purpose of the work is clearly to refresh the Catholic mind on the essentials of the deposit of faith. It is the work of the Church to teach the truth . . .

The present work is rich in quotations from Sacred Scripture and in citations from the Magisterium. The reader is consequently assured that he is being offered not the personal opinions of one man, but the tradition of Catholicism.

Mother Teresa has also written some comments on the Catechism in the front of the book under the heading, 'For All Who Use This Book'. She says:

> This catechism is a clear exposition of the teachings of the Church. It should be taught in schools and colleges, in religious formation programs, and in the family. Written in simple style, it is easy to understand, and it leaves no doubt in the mind as to what is required of us by the Church, as children of God and followers of Jesus Christ.

Appendix B

AUTHORITATIVE STATEMENTS OF ROMAN CATHOLIC TEACHING ON THE MASS

The Council of Trent

Session XXII: Doctrine on the Sacrifice of the Mass

Chapter I: On the institution of the most holy Sacrifice of the Mass

Forasmuch as, under the former Testament, according to the testimony of the Apostle Paul, there was no *perfection, because of the weakness of the Levitical priesthood*; there was need, God, the Father of mercies, so ordaining, that *another priest should rise, according to the order of Melchisedech*, our Lord Jesus Christ, who might consummate, and lead to what is perfect, as many as were to be sanctified. He, therefore, our God and Lord, though he was about to offer himself once on the altar of the cross unto God the Father, *by means of his death*, there to operate *an eternal redemption*; nevertheless, because that his priesthood was not to be extinguished by his death, in the Last Supper, on the night in which he was betrayed, – that he might leave, to his own beloved Spouse the Church, a visible sacrifice, such as the nature of man requires, whereby that bloody sacrifice, once to be accomplished on the cross, might be represented, and the memory thereof remain even unto the end of the world, and its salutary virtue be applied to the remission of those sins which we daily commit, – declaring himself constituted *a priest forever, according to the order of Melchisedech*, he offered up to God the Father his own body and blood under the species of bread and wine; and, under the symbols of those same things, he delivered [his own body and blood] to be received by his apostles, whom he then constituted priests of the New Testament; and by those words, *Do this in commemoration of me*, he commanded them and their successors in the priesthood to offer [them]; even as the Catholic Church has always understood and taught.

Chapter II: That the Sacrifice of the Mass is propitiatory, both for the living and the dead

And forasmuch as, in this divine sacrifice which is celebrated in the mass, that same Christ is contained and immolated in an unbloody manner who once offered himself in a bloody manner on the altar of the cross; the holy Synod teaches, that this sacrifice is truly propitiatory, and that by means thereof this is effected, that we obtain mercy, and find grace *in seasonable aid*, if we draw nigh unto God, contrite and penitent, with a sincere heart and upright faith, with fear and reverence. For the Lord, appeased by the oblation thereof, and granting the grace and gift of penitence, forgives even heinous crimes and sins. For the victim is one and the same, the same now offering by the ministry of priests, who then offered himself on the cross, the manner alone of offering being different. The fruits indeed of which oblation, of that bloody one to wit, are received most plentifully through this unbloody one; so far is this [latter] from derogating in any way from that [former oblation]. Wherefore, not only for the sins, punishments, satisfactions, and other necessities of the faithful who are living, but also for those who are departed in Christ, and who are not as yet fully purified, is it rightly offered, agreeably to a tradition of the apostles.

On the Sacrifice of the Mass

Canon I. If any one saith, that in the mass a true and proper sacrifice is not offered to God; or, that to be offered is nothing else but that Christ is given us to eat: let him be anathema.

Canon II. If any one saith, that by those words, *Do this for the commemoration of me* (Luke xxii. 19), Christ did not institute the apostles priests; or, did not ordain that they and other priests should offer his own body and blood: let him be anathema.

Canon III. If any one saith, that the sacrifice of the mass is only a sacrifice of praise and of thanksgiving; or, that it is a bare commemoration of the sacrifice consummated on the cross, but not a propitiatory sacrifice; or, that it profits him only who receives; and that it ought not to be offered for the living and the dead for sins, pains, satisfactions, and other necessities: let him be anathema.

Canon V. If any one saith, that it is an imposture to celebrate masses in honor of the saints, and for obtaining their intercession with God, as the Church intends: let him be anathema.

Canon VI. If any one saith, that the canon of the mass contains errors, and is therefore to be abrogated: let him be anathema.

The Documents of Vatican II

As often as the sacrifice of the cross in which 'Christ, our passover, has been sacrificed' (1 Cor. 5:7) is celebrated on an altar, the work of our redemption is carried on (p. 16).

In discharging their duty to sanctify their people, pastors should arrange for the celebration of the Eucharistic Sacrifice to be the center and culmination of the whole life of the Christian community (p. 418).

Through the hands of priests and in the name of the whole Church, the Lord's sacrifice is offered in the Eucharist in an unbloody and sacramental manner until He Himself returns (p. 535).

Christ is always present in His Church, especially in her liturgical celebrations. He is present in the sacrifice of the Mass, not only in the person of His minister, 'the same one now offering, through the ministry of priests, who formerly offered himself on the cross,' but especially under the Eucharistic species (pp. 140–41).

Thus the Eucharistic Action is the very heartbeat of the congregation of the faithful over which the priest presides. So priests must instruct them to offer to God the Father the divine Victim in the sacrifice of the Mass, and to join to it the offering of their own lives (p. 542).

At the Last Supper, on the night when He was betrayed, our Savior instituted the Eucharistic Sacrifice of His Body and Blood. He did this in order to perpetuate the sacrifice of the Cross throughout the centuries until He should come again, and so to intrust to His beloved spouse, the Church, a memorial of His death and resurrection: a sacrament of love, a sign of unity, a bond of charity, a paschal banquet in which Christ is consumed, the mind is filled with grace, and a pledge of future glory is given to us (p. 154).

The Code of Canon Law

Canon 897. The eucharistic Sacrifice, the memorial of the death and resurrection of the Lord, in which the Sacrifice of the cross is forever perpetuated, is the summit and the source of all worship and christian life.

Canon 904. Remembering always that in the mystery of the eucharistic Sacrifice the work of redemption is continually being carried out, priests are to celebrate frequently. Indeed, daily celebration is earnestly recommended, because, even if it should not be possible to have the faithful present, it is an action of Christ and of the Church in which priests fulfil their principal role.

Canon 906. A priest may not celebrate the eucharistic Sacrifice without the participation of at least one of the faithful, unless there is a good and reasonable cause for doing so.

The Question and Answer Catholic Catechism

1264. How is the Sacrifice of the Cross continued on earth?

The Sacrifice of the Cross is continued on earth through the Sacrifice of the Mass.

1265. What is the Sacrifice of the Mass?

The Sacrifice of the Mass is the true and properly called Sacrifice of the New Law. It is the Sacrifice in which Christ is offered under the species of bread and wine in an unbloody manner. The Sacrifice of the altar, then, is no mere empty commemoration of the Passion and Death of Jesus Christ, but a true and proper act of sacrifice. Christ, the eternal High Priest, in an unbloody way offers himself a most acceptable Victim to the eternal Father, as he did upon the Cross.

1268. How are the Mass and Calvary related?

The Mass and Calvary are related in three ways: as re-presentation, as memorial, and as an effective application to mankind of the merits gained by Christ's Death on the Cross.

1269. How does the Mass re-present Calvary?

The Mass re-presents Calvary by continuing Christ's sacrifice of himself to his heavenly Father. In the Mass, no less than on Calvary, Jesus really offers his life to his heavenly Father. This is possible because in the Mass is the same priest, Jesus Christ, who with his human will (united to the divine) offers himself; and it is the same victim, Jesus Christ, whose human life (united with the divinity) is sacrificed. The only difference is that, being now glorified, Christ cannot die a physical death as he did on the Cross. St Paul writes of Christ's self-offering: 'Since men only die once, and after that comes judgment, so Christ, too, offers himself only once to take the faults of many on himself'. (Hebrews 9:27–28).

1277. Does the Mass detract from the one, unique Sacrifice of the Cross?

The Mass in no way detracts from the one, unique Sacrifice of the Cross because the Mass is the same Sacrifice as that of the Cross, to continue on earth until the end of time. Christ not only was the priest who offered himself to his heavenly Father. He is the priest whose intercession for sinful mankind continues, only now he communicates the graces he had won for us by his bloody Passion and Death. The Mass, therefore, no less than the Cross, is expiatory for sins; but now the expiation is experienced by those for whom, on the Cross, the title of God's mercy had been gained.

1279. How are the merits of Calvary dispensed through the Holy Sacrifice of the Mass?

The merits of Calvary are dispensed through the Mass in that the graces Christ gained for us on the Cross are communicated by the Eucharistic Sacrifice.

1289. What are the graces conferred by the Mass as a sacrament?

The graces conferred by the Mass as a sacrament are twofold. Through the Mass we obtain forgiveness for venial sins and the remission of temporal punishment still due for past sins; we also obtain for ourselves and others the grace of repentance and the desire to expiate offenses against God. Looking to the future, the Mass is the single most effective source of grace by which Christ distributes the blessings of Calvary.

1294. Is the Sacrifice of the Mass of infinite value?

The Sacrifice of the Mass is of infinite value, no less than that of the Cross.

Appendix C

AUTHORITATIVE STATEMENTS OF ROMAN CATHOLIC TEACHING ON THE PRIESTHOOD

The Council of Trent

Session XXIII: The True and Catholic Doctrine concerning the Sacrament of Order

Chapter I: On the institution of the Priesthood of the New Law

Sacrifice and priesthood are, by the ordinance of God, in such wise conjoined, as that both have existed in every law. Whereas, therefore, in the New Testament, the Catholic Church has received, from the institution of Christ, the holy visible sacrifice of the Eucharist; it must needs also be confessed, that there is, in that Church, a new, visible, and external priesthood, into which the old has been *translated*. And the sacred Scriptures show, and the tradition of the Catholic Church has always taught, that this priesthood was instituted by the same Lord our Saviour, and that to the Apostles, and their successors in the priesthood, was the power delivered of consecrating, offering, and administering his body and blood, as also of forgiving and of retaining sins.

On the Sacrament of Order

Canon I. If any one saith, that there is not in the New Testament a visible and external priesthood; or, that there is not any power of consecrating and offering the true body and blood of the Lord, and of forgiving and retaining sins, but only an office and bare ministry of preaching the Gospel; or, that those who do not preach are not priests at all: let him be anathema.

Canon III. If any one saith, that order, or sacred ordination, is not truly and properly a sacrament instituted by Christ the Lord; or, that it is a kind of human figment devised by men unskilled in ecclesiastical matters; or, that it is only a kind of rite for choosing ministers of the Word of God and of the sacraments: let him be anathema.

Session XXII: Doctrine on the Sacrifice of the Mass

Chapter I: On the institution of the most holy Sacrifice of the Mass

He, therefore, our God and Lord, though he was about to offer himself once on the altar of the cross unto God the Father, *by means of his death*, there to operate *an eternal redemption*; nevertheless, because that his priesthood was not to be extinguished by his death, in the Last Supper, on the night in which he was betrayed, – that he might leave, to his own beloved Spouse the Church, a visible sacrifice, such as the nature of man requires, whereby that bloody sacrifice, once to be accomplished on the cross, might be represented, and the memory thereof remain even unto the end of the world, and its salutary virtue be applied to the remission of those sins which we daily commit, – declaring himself constituted *a priest forever, according to the order of Melchisedech*, he offered up to God the Father his own body and blood under the species of bread and wine; and, under the symbols of those same things, he delivered [his own body and blood] to be received by his apostles, whom he then constituted priests of the New Testament; and by those words, *Do this in commemoration of me*, he commanded them and their successors in the priesthood to offer [them]; even as the Catholic Church has always understood and taught.

On the Sacrifice of the Mass

Canon II. If any one saith, that by those words, *Do this for the commemoration of me* (Luke xxii. 19), Christ did not institute the apostles priests; or, did not ordain that they and other priests should offer his own body and blood: let him be anathema.

The Documents of Vatican II

Now, the same Lord has established certain ministers among the faithful in order to join them together in one body where 'all the members have not the same function' (Rom. 12:4). These ministers in the society of the faithful would be able by the sacred power of their order to offer sacrifice and to remit sins. They would perform their priestly office publicly for men in the name of Christ (p. 534).

Priests are taken from among men and appointed for men in the things which pertain to God, in order to offer gifts and sacrifices for sins . . .

By their vocation and ordination, priests of the New Testament are indeed set apart in a certain sense within the midst of God's people (p. 536).

Priests fulfill their chief duty in the mystery of the Eucharistic Sacrifice. In it the work of our redemption continues to be carried out (p. 560).

The pivotal principle on which the Council's teaching turns is that the priest is a man drawn from the ranks of the People of God to be made, in the very depths of his being, like to Christ, the Priest of mankind. He is consecrated by a special seal of the Holy Spirit. In virtue of this consecration, he acts in the person of Christ, and, as a minister of Christ, the Head, he is deputed to serve the People of God. Through him Christ continues and fulfills that mission which He received from the Father (p. 527).

Therefore, while it indeed presupposes the sacraments of Christian initiation, the sacerdotal office of priests is conferred by that special sacrament through which priests, by the anointing of the Holy Spirit, are marked with a special character and are so configured to Christ the Priest that they can act in the person of Christ the Head (p. 535).

The Code of Canon Law

Canon 900. The only minister who, in the person of Christ, can bring into being the sacrament of the Eucharist, is a validly ordained priest.

Canon 1008. By divine institution some among Christ's faithful are, through the sacrament of order, marked with an indelible character and are thus constituted sacred ministers; thereby they are consecrated and deputed so that, each according to his own grade, they fulfil, in the person of Christ the Head, the offices of teaching, sanctifying and ruling, and so they nourish the people of God.

The Question and Answer Catholic Catechism

1464. What is the sacrament of orders?

Orders is a sacrament of the New Law by which a share in the spiritual powers of Christ's ministry is conferred together with the grace to perform worthily the duties of one's office in the Church.

1465. What is the basis for the sacrament?

The basis for the sacrament of orders is Christ's own priestly ministry on earth, and the revealed fact that he associated others with him to learn his teachings, acquire his spirit, receive his powers, and thus continue his work of salvation until the end of time.

1466. When did Christ institute the sacrament of orders?

Christ actually instituted the sacrament of orders at the Last Supper. After he had consecrated the bread and wine, and changed them into his own body and blood, he told the apostles to 'do this as a memorial of me' (Luke 22:19). By this he was conferring on the apostles and their successors the principal power of this sacrament, namely to consecrate and offer his body and blood in the Sacrifice of the Mass.

1488. What is the primary ministry of a priest?

The primary ministry of a priest is to consecrate and offer the Holy Eucharist, and to forgive sins. In this, priests differ from deacons who do not receive the power to consecrate the Eucharist, offer Mass, or forgive sins by sacramental absolution.

Appendix D

AUTHORITATIVE STATEMENTS OF ROMAN CATHOLIC TEACHING ON CONFESSION AND PENANCE

The Council of Trent

Session XIV: On the Most Holy Sacraments of Penance and Extreme Unction

Chapter I: On the necessity, and on the institution of the Sacrament of Penance

If such, in all the regenerate, were their gratitude towards God, as that they constantly preserved the justice received in baptism by his bounty and grace, there would not have been need for another sacrament, besides that of baptism itself, to be instituted for the remission of sins. But because God, *rich in mercy, knows our frame*, he hath bestowed a remedy of life even on those who may, after baptism, have delivered themselves up to the servitude of sin and the power of the devil, – the sacrament to wit of Penance, by which the benefit of the death of Christ is applied to those who have fallen after baptism. Penitence was indeed at all times necessary, in order to attain to grace and justice, for all men who had defiled themselves by any mortal sin, even for those who begged to be washed by the sacrament of Baptism; that so, their perverseness renounced and amended, they might, with a hatred of sin and a godly sorrow of mind, detest so great an offense of God. Wherefore the prophet says: *Be con-*

verted and do penance for all your iniquities, and iniquity shall not be your ruin. The Lord also said: *Except you do penance, you shall also likewise perish*; and Peter, the prince of the apostles, recommending penitence to sinners who were about to be initiated by baptism, said: *Do penance, and be baptized every one of you.* Nevertheless, neither before the coming of Christ was penitence a sacrament, nor is it such, since his coming, to any previously to baptism. But the Lord then principally instituted the sacrament of penance, when, being raised from the dead, he breathed upon his disciples, saying: *Receive ye the Holy Ghost: whose sins you shall forgive, they are forgiven them, and whose sins you shall retain, they are retained.* By which action so signal, and words so clear, the consent of all the Fathers has ever understood that the power of *forgiving and retaining sins* was communicated to the apostles and their lawful successors, for the reconciling of the faithful who have fallen after baptism. And the Catholic Church with great reason repudiated and condemned as heretics the Novatians, who of old obstinately denied that power of forgiving. Wherefore, this holy Synod, approving of and receiving as most true this meaning of those words of our Lord, condemns the fanciful interpretations of those who, in opposition to the institution of this sacrament, falsely wrest those words to the power of preaching the Word of God, and of announcing the Gospel of Christ.

Chapter III: On the parts and on the fruit of this sacrament

The holy Synod doth furthermore teach, that the form of the sacrament of Penance, wherein its force principally consists, is placed in those words of the minister: *I absolve thee*, etc.; to which words indeed certain prayers are, according to the custom of holy Church, laudably joined, which nevertheless by no means regard the essence of that form, neither are they necessary for the administration of the sacrament itself. But the acts of the penitent himself, to wit, contrition, confession, and satisfaction, are as it were the matter of this sacrament. Which acts, inasmuch as they are, by God's institution, required in the penitent for the integrity of the sacrament, and for the full and perfect remission of sins, are for this reason called the parts of penance. But the thing signified indeed, and the effect of this sacrament, as far as regards its force and efficacy, is reconciliation with God, which sometimes, in persons who are pious and who receive this sacrament with devotion, is wont to be followed by peace and serenity of conscience, with exceeding consolation of spirit.

Chapter V: On Confession

From the institution of the sacrament of Penance, as already explained, the universal Church has always understood that the entire confession of sins was also instituted by the Lord, and is of divine right necessary for all who have fallen after baptism; because that our Lord Jesus Christ, when about to ascend from earth to heaven, left priests his own vicars, as presidents and judges, unto whom all the mortal crimes, into which the faithful of Christ may have fallen, should be carried, in order that, in accordance with the power of the keys, they may pronounce the sentence of forgiveness or retention of sins. For it is manifest that priests could not have exercised this judgment without knowledge of the cause; neither indeed could they have observed equity in enjoining punishments, if the said faithful should have declared their sins in general only, and not rather specifically, and one by one. Whence it is gathered that all the mortal sins, of which, after a diligent examination of themselves, they are conscious, must needs be by penitents enumerated in confession, even though those sins be most hidden, and committed only against the last two precepts of the decalogue, – sins which sometimes wound the soul more grievously, and are more dangerous, than those which are committed outwardly. For venial sins, whereby we are not excluded from the grace of God, and into which we fall more frequently, although they be rightly and profitably, and without any presumption, declared in confession, as the custom of pious persons demonstrates, yet may they be omitted without guilt, and be expiated by many other remedies. But, whereas all mortal sins, even those of thought, render men *children of wrath*, and enemies of God, it is necessary to seek also for the pardon of them all from God, with an open and modest confession.

Chapter VI: On the ministry of this sacrament, and on Absolution

But, as regards the minister of this sacrament, the holy Synod declares all those doctrines to be false, and utterly alien from the truth of the Gospel, which perniciously extend the ministry of the keys to any others soever besides bishops and priests; imagining, contrary to the institution of this sacrament, that those words of our Lord, *Whatsoever you shall bind upon earth, shall be bound also in heaven, and whatsoever you shall loose upon earth shall be loosed also in heaven*, and, *Whose sins you shall forgive, they are forgiven them, and whose sins you shall retain, they are retained*, were in such wise addressed to all the faithful of Christ indifferently and indiscriminately, as that everyone has the power of forgiving sins, – public sins to wit by rebuke, provided he that is rebuked shall acquiesce, and secret sins by a voluntary confession made to any individual whatsoever. It also teaches, that even priests, who are in mortal sin, exercise, through the virtue of the Holy Ghost which was bestowed in ordination, the office of forgiving sins, as the ministers of Christ; and that their sentiment is erroneous who contend that this power exists not in bad priests. But although the absolution of the priest is the dispensation of another's bounty, yet is it not a bare ministry only, whether of announcing the Gospel, or of declaring that sins are forgiven, but is after the manner of a judicial act, whereby sentence is pronounced by the priest as by a judge; and therefore the penitent ought not so to confide in his own personal faith as to think that, – even though there be no contrition on his part, or no intention on the part of the priest of acting seriously and absolving truly, – he is nevertheless truly and in God's sight absolved, on account of his faith alone. For neither would faith without penance bestow any remission of sins, nor would he be otherwise than most careless of his own salvation, who, knowing that a priest but absolved him in jest, should not carefully seek for another who would act in earnest.

Chapter VIII: On the necessity and on the fruit of Satisfaction

. . . the holy Synod declares, that it is wholly false, and alien from the Word of God, that the guilt is never forgiven by the Lord, without the whole punishment also being therewith pardoned . . . And it beseems the divine clemency, that sins be not in such wise pardoned us without any satisfaction, as that, taking occasion therefrom, thinking sins less grievous, we, offering as it were an insult and an *outrage to the Holy Ghost*, should fall into more grievous sins, *treasuring up wrath against the day of wrath*. For, doubtless, these satisfactory punishments greatly recall from sin, and check as it were with a bridle, and make penitents more cautious and watchful for the future.

Chapter IX: On works of Satisfaction

The Synod teaches furthermore, that so great is the liberality of the divine munificence, that we are able through Jesus Christ to make satisfaction to God the Father, not only by punishments voluntarily undertaken of ourselves for the punishment of sin, or by those imposed at the discretion of the priest according to the measure of our delinquency, but also, which is a very great proof of love, by the temporal scourges inflicted of God, and borne patiently by us.

On the Most Holy Sacrament of Penance

Canon VI. If any one denieth, either that sacramental confession was instituted, or is necessary to salvation, of divine right; or saith, that the manner of confessing secretly to a priest alone, which the Church hath ever observed from the beginning, and doth observe, is alien from the institution and command of Christ, and is a human invention: let him be anathema.

Canon VII. If any one saith, that, in the sacrament of Penance, it is not necessary, of divine right, for the remission of sins, to confess all and singular mortal sins which after due and diligent previous meditation are remembered, even those [mortal sins] which are secret, and those that are opposed to the two last commandments of the Decalogue, as also the circumstances which change the species of a sin; but [saith] that such confession is only useful to instruct and console the penitent, and that it was of old only observed in order to impose a canonical satisfaction; or saith that they, who strive to confess all their sins, wish to leave nothing to the divine mercy to pardon; or, finally, that it is not lawful to confess venial sins: let him be anathema.

Canon IX. If any one saith, that the sacramental absolution of the priest is not a judicial act, but a bare ministry of pronouncing and declaring sins to be forgiven to him who confesses; provided only he believe himself to be absolved, or [even though] the priest absolve not in earnest, but in joke; or saith, that the confession of the penitent is not required, in order that the priest may be able to absolve him: let him be anathema.

Canon XII. If any one saith, that God always remits the whole punishment together with the guilt, and that the satisfaction of penitents is no other than the faith whereby they apprehend that Christ has satisfied for them: let him be anathema.

Canon XIII. If any one saith, that satisfaction for sins, as to their temporal punishment, is nowise made to God, through the merits of Jesus Christ, by the punishments inflicted by him, and patiently borne, or by those enjoined by the priest, nor even by those voluntarily undertaken, as by fastings, prayers, alms-deeds, or by other works also of piety; and that, therefore, the best penance is merely a new life: let him be anathema.

Canon XIV. If any one saith, that the satisfactions, by which penitents redeem their sins through Jesus Christ, are not a worship of God, but traditions of men, which obscure the doctrine of grace, and the true worship of God, and the benefit itself of the death of Christ: let him be anathema.

The Documents of Vatican II

Those who approach the sacrament of penance obtain pardon from the mercy of God for offenses committed against Him (p. 28).

By the sacrament of penance sinners are reconciled to God and the Church (p. 541).

The Code of Canon Law

Canon 959. In the sacrament of penance the faithful who confess their sins to a lawful minister, are sorry for those sins and have a purpose of amendment, receive from God, through the absolution given by that minister, forgiveness of sins they have committed after baptism, and at the same time they are reconciled with the Church, which by sinning they wounded.

Canon 960. Individual and integral confession and absolution constitute the sole ordinary means by which a member of the faithful who is conscious of grave sin is reconciled with God and with the Church.

Canon 965. Only a priest is the minister of the sacrament of penance.

Canon 966. 1. For the valid absolution of sins, it is required that, in addition to the power of order, the minister has the faculty to exercise that power in respect of the faithful to whom he gives absolution.

2. A priest can be given this faculty either by the law itself, or by a concession issued by the competent authority in accordance with canon 969.

The Question and Answer Catholic Catechism

1318. What is penance?

Penance means repentance or satisfaction for sin. It is also a virtue, and one of the sacraments instituted by Christ.

1319. What is the virtue of penance?

Penance is the supernatural virtue that inclines a person to detest his sins because they have offended a loving God and deserved his just punishment, to firmly resolve not to commit these sins again, and to make satisfaction for one's offenses against God.

1320. Why is the virtue of penance necessary?

The virtue of penance is necessary for a sinner to be reconciled with God. If we expect his forgiveness, we must repent. Penance is also necessary because we must expiate and make reparation for the punishment which is due for our sins. That is why Christ tells us, 'Unless you repent you will all perish' (Luke 13:5).

1321. What is the sacrament of penance?

Penance is the sacrament instituted by Christ in which sinners are reconciled with God through the absolution of the priest.

1322. Why did Christ institute the sacrament of penance?

Christ instituted this sacrament to give us a ready and assured means of obtaining remission for the sins committed after baptism.

1326. What is the matter and form of the sacrament of penance?

The form of the sacrament is the words of absolution, which are said orally by an authorized priest. Essential for absolution are the words 'I absolve you from your sins.' The matter of the sacrament is the required acts of the penitent, namely, contrition, confession, and satisfaction.

1341. Can venial sin be forgiven even though mortal sins are not forgiven?

Venial sins cannot be forgiven if mortal sins have not been remitted. A person must be in the state of grace to merit divine mercy for his venial sins.

1368. Why is personal, specific confession necessary?

Personal, specific confession (called auricular confession) is necessary because this was taught by Christ. He gave his apostles and their successors the power to forgive sins, but also to not forgive them, implying that the faithful had to tell their sins in order for the priest to judge whether they should be absolved.

1381. What does the priest say after he gives absolution?

After giving absolution, he says, 'Give thanks to the Lord, for he is good.' The penitent concludes, 'His mercy endures forever.' Before dismissing the penitent, the priest recites one of several prayers, of which the best known is a plea for divine mercy, 'May the Passion of our Lord Jesus Christ, the merits of the Blessed Virgin Mary and of all the saints, and also whatever good you do and evil you endure, be cause for the remission of your sins, the increase of grace, and the reward of everlasting life. Amen.'

1382. Why does the priest assign a special penance to be said or done after confession?

The priest assigns this penance as partial satisfaction for the sins that were confessed and remitted.

1386. Why must satisfaction be made for sins already forgiven?

Satisfaction must be made for sins already forgiven because normally some – and even considerable – temporal punishment is still due, although the guilt has been removed.

1387. How do we know that temporal punishment may still be due after sins have been forgiven?

It has been the Church's constant teaching that guilt of sins can be removed and yet temporal punishment may still be due. The doctrine is based on divine revelation and underlies the Church's whole penitential discipline, including the practice of granting partial or plenary indulgences.

1389. How is satisfaction expiatory?

Satisfaction is expiatory by making up for the failure in love of God which is the root cause of sin, by voluntarily suffering to make up for self-indulgence, and by enduring pain in reparation for the harm or disorder caused by the commission of sin.

1390. How is satisfaction remedial?

Satisfaction is remedial by meriting grace from God to enlighten and strengthen a person against the same sins in the future.

1392. How can we make satisfactions for our sins?

We make satisfaction for our sins by every good act we perform in the state of grace, but especially by prayer, penance, and the practice of charity. While all prayer merits satisfaction for sin, it is most effective when we ask God to have mercy on us, and unite our prayers with voluntary self-denial. Penance for sin is not only bodily, like fast and abstinence, but also spiritual, like restraining curiosity or conversation and avoiding otherwise legitimate recreation. Moreover, the patient acceptance of trials or humiliations sent by God is expiatory. Finally, the practice of charity toward others is a powerful satisfaction for our lack of charity toward God. 'Above all,' we are told, 'Never let your love for each other grow insincere, since love covers over many a sin' (1 Peter 4:8).

1394. What is sacramental satisfaction?

Sacramental satisfaction is the penitential work imposed by a confessor in the confessional in order to make up for the injury done to God and atone for the temporal punishment due to sin already forgiven. The penitent is obliged to perform the penance imposed by the priest, and deliberate failure to perform a penance imposed for mortal sin is gravely sinful.

1395. What is extra-sacramental satisfaction?

Extra-sacramental satisfaction is every form of expiation offered to God outside the sacrament of penance. Our works of satisfaction are meritorious if they are done while in the state of grace and in a spirit of penance.

1400. How can we make up for sin?

We can make up for sin through the sorrows and trials of life, including the pain of death, or through the purifying penalties in the life beyond. Sin can also be expiated through indulgences.

1401. What is an indulgence?

An indulgence is the remission through the merits of Christ and his Church of the temporal punishment still due to forgiven sins.

1402. How do indulgences remove temporal punishment?

Indulgences remove temporal punishment through the Church's right to dispose the merits of Christ to her members. The Savior won the graces of expiation for sinners by His Passion and Death. The Church administers these benefits in consideration of the prayers and good works performed by the faithful.

Appendix E

AUTHORITATIVE STATEMENTS OF ROMAN CATHOLIC TEACHING ON THE EUCHARIST

The Council of Trent

Session XIII: Decree concerning the Most Holy Sacrament of the Eucharist

Chapter I: On the real presence of our Lord Jesus Christ in the most holy sacrament of the Eucharist

In the first place, the holy Synod teaches, and openly and simply professes, that, in the august sacrament of the holy Eucharist, after the consecration of the bread and wine, our Lord Jesus Christ, true God and man, is truly, really, and substantially contained under the species of those sensible things.

Chapter III: On the excellency of the most holy Eucharist over the rest of the sacraments

And this faith has ever been in the Church of God, that, immediately after the consecration, the veritable body of our Lord, and his veritable blood, together with his soul and divinity, are under the species of bread and wine . . . Wherefore it is most true, that as much is contained under either species as under both; for Christ whole and entire is under the species of bread, and under any part whatsoever of that species; likewise the whole (Christ) is under the species of wine, and under the parts thereof.

Chapter IV: On Transubstantiation

And because that Christ, our Redeemer, declared that which he offered under the species of bread to be truly his own body, therefore has it ever been a firm belief in the Church of God, and this holy Synod doth now declare it anew, that, by the consecration of the bread and of the wine, a conversion is made of the whole substance of the bread into the substance of the body of Christ our Lord, and of the whole substance of the wine into the substance of his blood; which conversion is, by the holy Catholic Church, suitably and properly called Transubstantiation.

Chapter V: On the cult and veneration to be shown to this most holy sacrament

Wherefore, there is no room left for doubt, that all the faithful of Christ may, according to the custom ever received in the Catholic Church, render in veneration the worship of latria, which is due to the true God, to this most holy sacrament. For not therefore is it the less to be adored on this account, that it was instituted by Christ, the Lord, in order to be received; for we believe the same God to be present therein, of whom the eternal Father, when introducing him into the world, says: *And let all the angels of God adore him*, whom the Magi, *falling down, adored*; who, in fine, as the Scripture testifies, was adored by the apostles in Galilee.

On the Most Holy Sacrament of the Eucharist

Canon I. If any one denieth, that, in the sacrament of the most holy Eucharist, are contained truly, really, and substantially, the body and blood together with the soul and divinity of our Lord Jesus Christ, and consequently the whole Christ; but saith that he is only therein as in a sign, or in figure, or virtue; let him be anathema.

Canon II. If any one saith, that, in the sacred and holy sacrament of the Eucharist, the substance of the bread and wine remains conjointly with the body and blood of our Lord Jesus Christ, and denieth that wonderful and singular conversion of the whole substance of the bread into the body, and of the whole substance of the wine into the blood – the species only of the bread and wine remaining – which conversion indeed the Catholic Church most aptly calls Transubstantiation: let him be anathema.

Canon VI. If any one saith, that, in the holy sacrament of the Eucharist, Christ, the only-begotten Son of God, is not to be adored with the worship, even external of latria; and is, consequently, neither to be venerated with a special festive solemnity, nor to be solemnly borne about in procession, according to the laudable and universal rite and custom of holy Church; or, is not to be proposed publicly to the people to be adored, and that the adorers thereof are idolators: let him be anathema.

Canon VIII. If any one saith, that Christ, given in the Eucharist, is eaten spiritually only, and not also sacramentally and really: let him be anathema.

The Documents of Vatican II

Christ is always present in His Church, especially in her liturgical celebrations. He is present in the sacrifice of the Mass, not only in the person of His minister, 'the same one now offering, through the ministry of priests, who formerly offered himself on the cross,' but especially under the Eucharistic species (pp. 140–41).

At the Last Supper, on the night when He was betrayed, our Savior instituted the Eucharistic Sacrifice of His Body and Blood. He did this in order to perpetuate the sacrifice of the Cross throughout the centuries until He should come again (p. 154).

In the house of prayer the most Holy Eucharist is celebrated and preserved. There the faithful gather, and find help and comfort through venerating the presence of the Son of God our Savior, offered for us on the sacrificial altar (p. 543).

The Code of Canon Law

Canon 897. The most venerable sacrament is the blessed Eucharist, in which Christ the Lord himself is contained, offered and received, and by which the Church continually lives and grows. The eucharistic Sacrifice, the memorial of the death and resurrection of the Lord, in which the Sacrifice of the cross is forever perpetuated, is the summit and the source of all worship and christian life.

Canon 898. Christ's faithful are to hold the blessed Eucharist in the highest honour. They should take an active part in the celebration of the most august Sacrifice of the Mass; they should receive the sacrament with great devotion and frequently, and should reverence it with the greatest adoration.

Canon 899. The celebration of the Eucharist is an action of Christ himself and of the Church. In it Christ the Lord, through the ministry of the priest, offers himself, substantially present under the appearances of bread and wine, to God the Father, and gives himself as spiritual nourishment to the faithful who are associated with him in his offering.

Canon 904. Remembering always that in the mystery of the eucharistic Sacrifice the work of redemption is continually being carried out, priests are to celebrate frequently.

The Question and Answer Catholic Catechism

1212. What is the center of the whole Catholic liturgy?

The center of the whole Catholic liturgy is the Eucharist. The Eucharist is most important in the life of the Church because it is Jesus Christ. It is the Incarnation continued in space and time. The other sacraments and all the Church's ministries and apostolates are directed toward the Eucharist.

1214. What is the sacrament of the Eucharist?

The Eucharist is a sacrament which really, truly, and substantially contains the body and blood, soul, and divinity of our Lord Jesus Christ under the appearances of bread and wine. It is the great sacrament of God's love in which Christ is eaten, the mind is filled with grace, and a pledge is given to us of future glory.

1217. Is the Eucharist necessary for salvation?

The Eucharist is necessary for salvation, to be received either sacramentally or in desire. Christ's words, 'if you do not eat the flesh of the Son of Man and drink his blood, you will not have life in you' (John 6:53), mean that Holy Communion is necessary to sustain the life of grace in a person who has reached the age of reason.

1219. What is contained in this sign?

After consecration, this sign contains the whole Christ, his body and blood, his soul and divinity.

1223. Is only the substance of Christ's human nature present in the Eucharist?

Christ is present in the Eucharist not only with everything that makes him man, but with all that makes him this human being. He is therefore present with all his physical properties, hands and feet and head and human heart. He is present with his human soul, with his thoughts, desires, and human affections.

1224. How does Christ become present in the Eucharist?

Christ becomes present in the Eucharist by means of transubstantiation. Transubstantiation is the term used to identify the change that takes place at the consecration.

1225. What remains of the bread and wine after consecration?

After the consecration, nothing remains of the bread and wine except their external properties. Their substance becomes the living body and blood of Christ.

1227. Is Jesus Christ present in the Eucharist as long as the species remain?

Yes, Jesus Christ is present in the Eucharist as long as the species remain. Therefore, we worship the Blessed Sacrament as we would worship the person of Jesus himself.

1228. Why is the Eucharist the most excellent of all the sacraments?

The Eucharist is the most excellent of all the sacraments because it contains Christ himself. All the other sacraments are channels of grace but they do not actually possess Jesus Christ, the Author of grace.

1239. What change takes place when the priest pronounces the words of consecration in the Mass?

When the priest pronounces the words of consecration, Jesus Christ becomes present on the altar at that very moment. We perceive the presence of Christ in the Eucharist by faith alone.

1240. How is the dogma of the Real Presence proved?

The dogma of the Real Presence is proved from Sacred Scripture, from Sacred Tradition, and from the infallible teaching of the Church.

Appendix F

AUTHORITATIVE STATEMENTS OF ROMAN CATHOLIC TEACHING ON BAPTISM

The Council of Trent

Session V: Decree concerning Original Sin

3. If any one asserts, that this sin of Adam, – which in its origin is one, and being transfused into all by propagation, not by imitation, is in each one as his own, – is taken away either by the powers of human nature, or by any other remedy than the merit of the *one mediator, our Lord Jesus Christ, who hath reconciled us to God in his own blood, being made unto us justice, sanctification, and redemption;* or if he denies that the said merit of Jesus Christ is applied, both to adults and to infants, by the sacrament of baptism rightly administered in the form of the Church; let him be anathema: *For there is no other name under heaven given to men, whereby we must be saved.* Whence that voice: *Behold the lamb of God, behold him who taketh away the sins of the world*; and that other: *As many as have been baptized, have put on Christ.*

4. If any one denies, that infants, newly born from their mothers' wombs, even though they be sprung from baptized parents, are to be baptized; or says that they are baptized indeed *for the remission of sins*, but that they derive nothing of original sin from Adam, which has need of being expiated by the laver of regeneration for obtaining life everlasting, – whence it follows as a consequence, that in them the form of

baptism, *for the remission of sins*, is understood to be not true, but false, – let him be anathema. For that which the apostle has said, *By one man sin entered into the world, and by sin death, and so death passed upon all men, in whom all have sinned*, is not to be understood otherwise than as the Catholic Church spread every where hath always understood it. For, by reason of this rule of faith, from a tradition of the apostles, even infants, who could not as yet commit any sin of themselves, are for this cause truly *baptized for the remission of sins*, that in them that may be cleansed away by regeneration, which they have contracted by generation. *For, unless a man be born again of water and the Holy Ghost, he can not enter into the kingdom of God.*

5. If any one denies, that, by the grace of our Lord Jesus Christ, which is conferred in baptism, the guilt of original sin is remitted; or even asserts that the whole of that which has the true and proper nature of sin is not taken away; but says that it is only rased, or not imputed: let him be anathema.

Session VII: On the Sacraments in General

Canon III. – If any one saith, that in the Roman Church, which is the mother anad mistress of all churches, there is not the true doctrine concerning the sacrament of baptism: let him be anathema.

Canon V. – If any one saith, that baptism is free, that is, not necessary unto salvation: let him be anathema.

The Documents of Vatican II

By the sacrament of baptism, whenever it is properly conferred in the way the Lord determined, and received with the appropriate dispositions of soul, a man becomes truly incorporated into the crucified and glorified Christ and is reborn to a sharing of the divine life, as the apostle says: 'For you were buried together with him in Baptism, and in him also rose again through faith in the working of God who raised him from the dead' (Col. 2:12; cf. Rom. 6:4).

Baptism, therefore, constitutes a sacramental bond of unity linking all who have been reborn by means of it (pp. 363–64).

For priests are brothers among brothers with all those who have been reborn at the baptismal font (p. 552).

Therefore, all must be converted to Him as He is made known by the Church's preaching. All must be incorporated into Him by baptism, and into the Church which is His body. For Christ Himself 'in explicit terms . . . affirmed the necessity of faith and baptism (cf. Mk. 16:16; Jn. 3:5) and thereby affirmed also the necessity of the Church, for through baptism as through a door men enter the Church. Whosoever, therefore, knowing that the Catholic Church was made necessary by God through Jesus Christ, would refuse to enter her or to remain in her could not be saved (p. 593).

The Code of Canon Law

Canon 849. Baptism, the gateway to the sacraments, is necessary for salvation, either by actual reception or at least by desire. By it people are freed from sins, are born again as children of God and, made like to Christ by an indelible character, are incorporated into the Church. It is validly conferred only by washing in real water with the proper form of words.

The Question and Answer Catholic Catechism

1140. What is baptism?

Baptism is the sacrament of spiritual rebirth. Through the symbolic action of washing with water and the use of appropriate ritual words, the baptized person is cleansed of all his sins and incorporated into Christ. It was foretold in Ezekiel, 'I shall pour clean water over you and you will be cleansed; I shall cleanse you of all your defilement and all your idols. I shall give you a new heart, and put a new spirit in you' (Ezekiel 36:25–26).

1151. What are the effects of baptism?

The effects of baptism are the removal of the guilt of sin and all punishment due to sin, conferral of the grace of regeneration and the infused virtues, incorporation into Christ and his Church, receiving the baptismal character and the right to heaven.

1152. What sins does baptism take away?

Baptism remits the guilt of all sins, that is, it takes away all sins, whether original sin as inherited from Adam at conception, or actual sin as incurred by each person on reaching the age of reason. No matter how frequent, or how grave the actual sins may be, their guilt is all removed at baptism. All of this is the pure gift of God, since St. Paul writes, 'It was for no reason except his own compassion that he saved us, by means of the cleansing water of rebirth' (Titus 3:5).

1153. What penalties does baptism remove?

Baptism removes all the penalties, eternal and temporal, attached to original and actual sin.

1155. What is the grace of regeneration?

The grace of regeneration infuses into our souls the life of the grace that Christ won for us by his Death and Resurrection. It is the new birth of which Christ spoke to Nicodemus (cf. John 3:3) and the new creation described by St. Paul (cf. 2 Corinthians 5:17).

1157. How does baptism incorporate us into Christ?

By baptism we become members of Christ's Mystical Body, which is the Church. That is why 'By the sacrament of baptism, whenever it is properly conferred in the way the Lord determined and received with the proper dispositions of soul, man becomes truly incorporated into the crucified and glorified Christ and is reborn to a sharing of the divine life, as the apostle says: "For you were buried together with him in baptism, and in him also rose again through faith in the working of God who raised him from the dead" (Rom. 6:4)' (Second Vatican Council, Decree on Ecumenism, 22).

Appendix G

AUTHORITATIVE STATEMENTS OF ROMAN CATHOLIC TEACHING ON SALVATION

The Council of Trent

Session VI: On Justification

Canon XXIV. If any one saith, that the justice received is not preserved and also increased before God through good works; but that the said works are merely the fruits and signs of Justification obtained, but not a cause of the increase thereof: let him be anathema.

Canon XXIX. If any one saith, that he who has fallen after baptism is not able by the grace of God to rise again; or, that he is able indeed to recover the justice which he has lost, but by faith alone without the sacrament of Penance, contrary to what the holy Roman and universal Church – instructed by Christ and his Apostles – has hitherto professed, observed, and taught: let him be anathema.

Canon XXX. If any one saith, that, after the grace of Justification has been received, to every penitent sinner the guilt is remitted, and the debt of eternal punishment is blotted out in such wise that there remains not any debt of temporal punishment to be discharged either in this world, or in the next in Purgatory, before the entrance to the kingdom of heaven can be opened [to him]: let him be anathema.

Canon XXXII. If any one saith, that the good works of one that is justified are in such manner the gifts of God, that they are not also the good merits of him that is justified; or, that the said justified, by the good works which he performs through the grace of God and the merit of Jesus Christ, whose living member he is, does not truly merit increase of grace, eternal life, and the attainment of that eternal life, – if so be, however, that he depart in grace, – and also an increase of glory: let him be anathema.

Session VII: On the Sacraments in General

Canon I. If any one saith, that the sacraments of the New Law were not all instituted by Jesus Christ, our Lord; or, that they are more, or less, than seven, to wit, Baptism, Confirmation, the Eucharist, Penance, Extreme Unction, Order, and Matrimony; or even that any of these seven is not truly and properly a sacrament: let him be anathema.

Canon IV. If any one saith, that the sacraments of the New Law are not necessary unto salvation, but superfluous; and that, without them, or without the desire thereof, men obtain of God, through faith alone, the grace of justification; – though all [the sacraments] are not indeed necessary for every individual: let him be anathema.

Canon VIII. If any one saith, that by the said sacraments of the New Law grace is not conferred through the act performed, but that faith alone in the divine promise suffices for the obtaining of grace: let him be anathema.

The Documents of Vatican II

This sacred Synod turns its attention first to the Catholic faithful. Basing itself upon sacred Scripture and tradition, it teaches that the Church, now sojourning on earth as an exile, is necessary for salvation. For Christ, made present to us in His body, which is the Church, is the one Mediator and the unique Way of salvation. In explicit terms He Himself affirmed the necessity of faith and baptism (cf. Mk. 16:16; John. 3:5) and thereby affirmed also the necessity of the

Church, for through baptism as through a door men enter the Church. Whosoever, therefore, knowing that the Catholic Church was made necessary by God through Jesus Christ, would refuse to enter her or to remain in her could not be saved (pp. 32–33).

The mission of the Church concerns the salvation of men, which is to be achieved by belief in Christ and by His grace. Hence the apostolate of the Church and of all her members is primarily designed to manifest Christ's message by words and deeds and to communicate His grace to the world. This work is done mainly through the ministry of the Word and of the sacraments, which are entrusted in a special way to the clergy (p. 496).

The Code of Canon Law

Canon 849. Baptism, the gateway to the sacraments, is necessary for salvation, either by actual reception or at least by desire. By it people are freed from sins, are born again as children of God and, made like to Christ by an indelible character, are incorporated into the Church. It is validly conferred only by a washing in real water with the proper form of words.

The Question and Answer Catholic Catechism

401. Why did Christ establish the Church?

Christ established the Church as a universal sacrament of salvation.

402. How is the Church the universal sacrament of salvation?

The Church is the universal sacrament of salvation as the divinely instituted means of conferring grace on all the members of the human family.

403. How does the Church communicate divine grace to mankind?

The Church communicates grace to mankind by her teaching of revealed truth, her celebration of Mass and administration of the sacraments, her prayers and the practice of virtue by her members, and her guidance and government of the faithful according to the will of God.

412. Is the Church necessary for salvation?

Yes, the Church is necessary for salvation. Christ himself declared that no one can be saved except through faith and baptism. He thereby affirmed the necessity of the Church, to which he entrusted the fullness of revelation and into which a person enters, as through a door, in the sacrament of baptism. Christ's words on this are clear, 'He who believes and is baptized will be saved; he who does not believe will be condemned' (Mark 16:16).

413. For whom is there no salvation outside the Church?

There is no salvation for those who, though incorporated into the Church by baptism, fail to persevere in sanctifying grace and die in the state of mortal sin. Those also are not saved who realize what they are doing but refuse to be baptized and accept the Church's means of salvation.

461. What does the Catholic Church believe about the forgiveness of sins?

She believes it is God's will that no one is forgiven except through the merits of Jesus Christ, and that these merits are uniquely channeled through the Church he founded. Consequently, even as the Church is the universal sacrament of salvation, she is also the universal sacrament of reconciliation.

462. How does the Church communicate the merits of Christ's mercy to sinners?

The Church communicates Christ's mercy to sinners through the Mass and the sacraments, and all the prayers and good works of the faithful.

463. What is the Church's role in the reconciliation of sinners to God?

The Church reconciles sinners to God mainly by her exercise of God's mercy, through the sacraments which he instituted.

1119. Are the sacraments necessary for salvation?

According to the way God has willed that we be saved, the sacraments are necessary for salvation.

492. Is faith in what God revealed sufficient for salvation?

No, we must also keep his Commandments. As Christ himself told us, 'If you wish to enter into life, keep the commandments' (Matthew 19:17).

493. How do we keep the commandments of God?

We keep the commandments of God by living a good moral life.

General Index

Extended treatment of various topics has been indicated by the use of **bold** type in the references.

Scripture Index

Wherever scripture texts have been used to support authoritative Roman Catholic teaching, this has been indicated in the index by italicising the reference.